Audition Speeches for Black, South Asian and Middle Eastern Actors
Monologues for Women

Audition Speeches for Black, South Asian and Middle Eastern Actors Monologues for Women

Edited by

SIMEILIA HODGE-DALLAWAY

Foreword by

Lolita Chakrabarti

Bloomsbury Methuen Drama
An imprint of Bloomsbury Publishing Plc

B L O O M S B U R Y

LONDON · OXFORD · NEW YORK · NEW DELHI · SYDNEY

Bloomsbury Methuen Drama

An imprint of Bloomsbury Publishing Plc

Imprint previously known as Methuen Drama

50 Bedford Square	1385 Broadway
London	New York
WC1B 3DP	NY 10018
UK	USA

www.bloomsbury.com

**BLOOMSBURY, METHUEN DRAMA and the Diana logo are trademarks of
Bloomsbury Publishing Plc**

First published 2016

British Library Cataloguing-in-Publication Data
A catalogue record for this book is available from the British Library

ISBN:	PB:	978-1-4742-2924-1
	ePDF:	978-1-4742-2925-8
	ePub:	978-1-4742-2926-5

Library of Congress Cataloging-in-Publication Data
A catalog record for this book is available from the Library of Congress

Cover design by Clare Turner

Typeset by Fakenham Prepress Solutions, Fakenham, Norfolk NR21 8NN
Printed and bound in Great Britain

We gratefully acknowledge financial assistance from the
Arts Council England and the National Lottery

This book is dedicated to my mother Charmaine Miller, sister Naomi Dallaway, cousin Cherene Miller and partner Reginald Edmund.

Rest in Eternal Peace
Uncle Jeremiah, Nanny Catherine and Junior Bertie

Contents

Thirties

Forties +

Foreword

I envy you this volume. Twenty-five years ago when I started acting there wasn't a book like this one. When I auditioned for drama school I had to find a classical and a modern piece. Following my drama teacher's advice I chose Goneril from *King Lear* and a middle-aged African American woman from Arthur Miller's *The American Clock*. I was seventeen. It was beautiful writing and pushed my acting abilities, but I made that choice because of a lack of options. I did not know where else to look.

This book gives you a huge head start. It is a signpost showing you what is out there and pointing the way to good stories by great writers with well-rounded female characters.

This is an important collection of monologues in a marketplace where women of colour are rarely centre stage. All too often we are background characters with minor voices, women who support the central narrative but have no real effect on its progress. Here, you have interesting, emotional, conflicted, humorous and fascinating women who are integral to the plot.

This is an essential resource for actresses who have the ability to play these roles. It's a great mark of your versatility as an actress to be able to play characters with different cultural identities. To be able to switch from Shakepeare's Juliet to Salima in *Ruined* by Lynn Nottage; from Anouilh's Antigone to Reema in *Khandan* by Gurpreet Kaur Bhatti; from Euripides' Medea to Angela in *Category B* by Roy Williams, requires true actorly transformation.

As I read the monologues in this book I was genuinely moved. These characters are singular windows into a fascinating array of cultures – women from all walks of life with whom we can empathise as their problems and flaws are revealed and explored. Drama allows us to travel without leaving our hometown. It personalizes stories from cultures we are not part of, offering a new understanding of people, values and morality from a different perspective. So with all that in mind, taking these words and making these people live is quite a responsibility!

Auditions are always hard because you have to sustain a dramatic narrative in your head while standing in a fully lit room before a panel that judges you. The more preparation you do, the easier it is. I always find it surprising when actors do not read the play from which their monologue is taken. The playwright has laced the story with everything you need to know about what motivates your character. The more you sit in your character through knowledge and study, the easier the playing becomes. And ultimately, knowing your character's impulses and desires will make the words your own.

In her introduction Simeilia Hodge-Dallaway says this 'is a celebration of a diverse range of captivating and truly memorable leading female characters'. I wholeheartedly agree. Enjoy them and speak loud! These are voices that need to be heard.

Lolita Chakrabarti
Playwright and actor

Performing Rights

Plc, 50 Bedford Square, London WC1B 3DP, performance.permissions@bloomsbury.com
Copyright © Sudha Bhuchar 2006

Crash by Pamela Mala Sinha
John Rait, A.C.I., 205 Ontario Street, Toronto, ON M5A 2V6, Canada
Copyright © Pamela Mala Sinha 2014. Reprinted with permission of J. Gordon Shillingford Publishing

A Day at the Racists by Anders Lustgarten
Curtis Brown Group Ltd., Haymarket House, 28–29 Haymarket, London SW1Y 4SP, info@curtisbrown.co.uk,
Copyright © Anders Lustgarten 2010

Desert Sunrise by Misha Shulman
Misha Shulman, 610 East 7th Street, 1B, Brooklyn, NY, 11218, USA
Excerpted from *Salaam, Peace: An Anthology of Middle Eastern-American Drama*. Copyright © Misha Shulman 2009. Reprinted by permission of Theatre Communications Group

The Fever Chart by Naomi Wallace
The Gersh Agency, 41 Madison Avenue, 33rd Floor, New York, NY 10010
Excerpted from *The Fever Chart: Three Visions of the Middle East*. Copyright © Naomi Wallace 2009. Reprinted by permission of Theatre Communications Group, Inc., 520 Eighth Avenue, 24th Floor, New York, NY 10018–4156

Fireworks by Dalia Taha
Casarotto Ramsay & Associates Ltd, Waverley House, 7–12 Noel Street, London W1F 8GQ, rights@casarotto.co.uk
Copyright © Dalia Taha 2015; translation copyright © Clem Naylor 2015

Fish Eyes Trilogy by Anita Majumdar
Playwrights Canada Press, 269 Richmond Street West, Suite 202, Toronto, Ontario, M5V 1X1, Canada, info@playwrightscanada.com
Excerpted from *Fish Eyes* by Anita Majumdar. Copyright © Anita Majumdar 2015. Reprinted by permission of Playwrights Canada Press

Harlem Duet by Djanet Sears
John Rait, A.C.I., 205 Ontario Street, Toronto, ON M5A 2V6, Canada
Copyright © Djanet Sears 1996. Reprinted with permission of J. Gordon Shillingford Publishing

The Hour of Feeling by Mona Mansour
The Gersh Agency, 41 Madison Avenue, 33rd Floor, New York, NY 10010, info@gershla.com
Copyright © Mona Mansour 2012

The House That Will Not Stand by Marcus Gardley
William Morris, 11 Madison Avenue, New York, NY 10010, USA
Copyright © Marcus Gardley 2014

Hurt Village by Katori Hall
Creative Artists Agency, 162 Fifth Avenue, 6th Floor, New York, NY 10010
Copyright © Katori Hall 2011

The Husbands by Sharmila Chauhan
Oberon Books Ltd, 521 Caledonian Road, London N7 9RH
Copyright © Sharmila Chauhan 2014. By kind permission of Oberon Books Ltd

I Just Stopped By To See The Man by Stephen Jeffreys
Nick Hern Books, The Glasshouse, 49a Goldhawk Road, London W12 8QP, rights@nickhernbooks.co.uk
Copyright © Stephen Jeffreys 2000. Reprinted by permission of Nick Hern Books: www.nickhernbooks.co.uk

In the Continuum by Danai Gurira & Nikkole Salter
United Talent Agency LLC, 9336 Civic Center Drive, Beverly Hills, CA 90210, mediarelations@unitedtalent.com
Copyright © Nikkole Salter and Danai Gurira 2012

Josephine and I by Cush Jumbo
By professionals to Curtis Brown Group Ltd., Haymarket House, 28–29 Haymarket, London SW1Y 4SP info@curtisbrown.co.uk, and by amateurs to Permissions Department, Methuen Drama, Bloomsbury Publishing Plc, 50 Bedford Square, London WC1B 3DP, performance.permissions@bloomsbury.com
Copyright © Cush Jumbo 2013

Khandan by Gurpreet Kaur Bhatti

Independent Talent Group, 40 Whitfield Street, London W1T 2RH
Copyright © Gurpreet Kaur Bhatti 2014. Reprinted by kind
permission of Oberon Books Ltd

Melody Loses Her Mojo by Keith Saha

By professionals to Sheil Land Associates Ltd., 52 Doughty Street,
London WC1N 2LS, info@sheilland.co.uk, and by amateurs to
Permissions Department, Methuen Drama, Bloomsbury Publishing
Plc, 50 Bedford Square, London WC1B 3DP, performance.permis-
sions@bloomsbury.com
Copyright © Keith Saha 2013

The Mountaintop by Katori Hall

Creative Artists Agency, 162 Fifth Avenue, 6th Floor, New York,
NY 10010
Copyright © Katori Hall 2011

My Name is … by Sudha Bhuchar

Tamasha, Rich Mix, 35–47 Bethnal Green Road, London E1 6LA,
admin@tamasha.org.uk
Copyright © Sudha Bhuchar 2014

9 Parts of Desire by Heather Raffo

AO International, 540 President St. Unit 2E, Brooklyn, NY 11215,
info@aoiagency.com
Copyright © Heather Raffo 2002. Reprinted by permission of
Northwestern University Press and Dramatists Play Service

Oh My Sweet Land by Amir Nizar Zuabi

Judy Daish Associates Limited, 2 St Charles Place, London W10
6EG, licensing@judydaish.com
Copyright © Amir Nizar Zuabi 2014

Rice Boy by Sunil Kuruvilla

Playwrights Canada Press, 269 Richmond Street West, Suite 202,
Toronto, Ontario, M5V 1X1, Canada, info@playwrightscanada.
com
Excerpted from *Rice Boy* by Sunil Kuruvilla. Copyright © Sunil
Kuruvilla 2009. Reprinted by permission of Playwrights Canada
Press

Ruined by Lynn Nottage
Creative Artists Agency, 162 Fifth Avenue, 6th Floor, New York, NY 10010
Excerpted from *Ruined* by Lynn Nottage. Copyright © Lynn Nottage 2009, 2010. Reprinted by permission of Nick Hern Books: www.nickhernbooks.co.uk

Shades by Alia Bano
The Agency (London) Ltd., 24 Pottery Lane, Holland Park, London W11 4LZ, info@theagency.co.uk
Copyright © Alia Bano 2009

Tamam by Betty Shamieh
Abrams Artists Agency, 275 Seventh Ave, 26th Floor, New York, NY 10001, USA
Copyright © Betty Shamieh 2001. Reprinted with permission from Betty Shamieh

The Usual Auntijies by Paven Virk
Alan Brodie Representation, Paddock Suite, The Courtyard, 55 Charterhouse Street, London EC1M 6HA, abr@alanbrodie.com
Copyright © Paven Virk 2011

We Are Proud to Present a Presentation About the Herero of Namibia, Formerly Known as Southwest Africa, From the German Sudwestafrika, Between the Years 1884–1915 by Jackie Sibblies Drury
AO International Agency, 540 President Street 2E, Brooklyn, NY 11215, info@aoiagency.com
Copyright © Jackie Sibblies Drury

Wedding Day at the Cro-Magnons by Wajdi Mouawad
Oberon Books Ltd, 521 Caledonian Road, London N7 9RH
Copyright © Wajdi Mouawad. Reprinted by kind permission of Oberon Books Ltd

The Westbridge by Rachel De-lahay
Alan Brodie Representation, Paddock Suite, The Courtyard, 55 Charterhouse Street, London EC1M 6HA, abr@alanbrodie.com
Copyright © Rachel De-lahay 2011

Every effort has been made to trace and acknowledge copyright owners. If any right has been omitted the publishers offer their apologies and will rectify this in subsequent editions following notification.

Introduction

We owe it to ourselves to never stop learning about the wealth of talent which exists in our neighbourhoods, in our cities and around the world – so that we can understand ourselves, our ancestry and our community to empower, grow, celebrate and cultivate new ideas. This was my self-written mantra which became the springboard to create this anthology of monologues for Black, South Asian and Middle Eastern actors.

After troubleshooting and managing the Black Play Archive at the National Theatre – a digital resource initiated by Kwame Kwei-Armah which consisted of professionally produced plays written by black British playwrights over the last seventy years – in addition to writing the first monologue anthology for black actors from black British plays, I had a strong desire to continue expanding my knowledge of plays for culturally diverse actors from British and international contemporary writers.

With the support of Arts Council England, I travelled to the USA and London to carry out research in order to gather the material for this anthology. At every stop off point, there was an immediate yet effortless ripple effect of communication, as the word about the forthcoming publication spread across the artistic communities internationally in person and over the internet, which enabled me to connect with practitioners, literary managers and producers based throughout London, Canada, New York, Chicago, Baltimore, Australia and Africa. I spent several months perusing personal and professional libraries, receiving recommendations from Kwame Kwei-Armah, Catherine Rodriguez, Gavin Witt, Betty Shamieh, Naomi Wallace, Ismail Khalidi, John Jack Patterson, Dalbir Singh and Raphael Martin, to name but a few. From practitioners, sales assistants at bookshops to audiences, everyone had a list of new, exciting and powerful contemporary plays which they urged me to read and select for this publication. Many of which are featured in this anthology, and the ones that never made the final draft have formed a place in my ever-growing play library, regularly feeding into the multiple programming conversations with directors and other theatre professionals.

Ironically, as I carried out the research for this collection from a place of celebration and love for my community, the same community was in uprising over the numerous accounts of the loss of innocent lives. This anthology was created against the backdrop of protests for social justice for Trayvon Martin, Michael Brown, Sandra Bland, the scarcely reported missing schoolgirls in Nigeria, the Charleston church shooting and the many innocent adults and children killed during the Israel–Gaza conflict – possibly, the most painful time I have ever experienced in my entire lifetime.

But as I read the works written by the ground-breaking contemporary writers featured in this anthology, it made sense of the chaos around me; suddenly these local and worldly events were more real and personal. The people who were reported in the media were three-dimensional with feelings, backstories and families. The world that they lived in was depicted through our five senses and imagination, instantly transporting us to somewhere tangible and coherent. There is something quite special about exploring the world through the voices of contemporary writers who have the power to portray the world as they see it, and thus influence, educate, challenge, changing the hearts and minds of their audience, bringing healing and comfort to the community.

Through this process, it became clear to me the power and importance of the role of a writer and the many reasons for us to champion writers; as the African American actress Viola Davis says, '[writers] redefine what it means to be beautiful, to be sexy, to be a leading woman and to be black'.

This anthology is a celebration of a diverse range of captivating and truly memorable leading female characters that represent all what we are, drawing on our culturally rich theatrical tradition of song, storytelling, dance and spirituality. These stories represent what it means to be a twenty-first-century woman of colour, in business, at war and in life. With monologues from Katori Hall, Cush Jumbo, Sabrina Mahfouz, Sudha Bhuchar, Betty Shamieh and Nadia Davids, the characters and themes are wide-ranging, featuring character journeys that cross cultural, political and historical boundaries.

The material has been arranged into age-specific groups: teens, twenties, thirties and forties-plus. Admittedly the playing age for some of the pieces were not specified for a particular age by the author of the play. Therefore, I would strongly encourage you to break convention and thus take a playful approach by reading monologues outside of your age category – you never know what you may discover.

For the purpose of this book, I have included plays which have been published to encourage readers to invest in the full-length version of the plays (please refer to the publication list on page 176). I hope these monologues will inspire you to read further and discover more about the playwrights and plays they come from.

Discovering the plays featured in this anthology has been a wonderful learning experience for me; I hope actors from all over the world will embrace and enjoy this exploration of voices, experiences and themes.

Teens

From

THE HOUSE THAT WILL NOT STAND

by Marcus Gardley

The world premiere of *The House That Will Not Stand* was
staged at the Berkeley Repertory Theatre on 31 January 2014,
directed by Patricia McGregor. This was subsequently followed
by a production at Tricycle Theatre in London on 9 October
2014, directed by Artistic Director Indhu Rusbasingham with
the following cast: Ayesha Antoine (Agnès), Ronke Adekoluejo
(Odette), Michele Austin (La Veuve), Martina Laird (Beartrice),
Tanya Moodie (Makeda), Clare Perkins (Marie Josephine),
Danusia Samal (Maude Lynn) and Paul Shelley (Monsieur L.
Albans).

The House That Will Not Stand is set in New Orleans, a southern
American state renowned for voodoo practices, haunted houses
and tormented souls. African American playwright Marcus
Gardley embraces the supernatural world to create a play which is
two-parts period drama and one-part harrowing ghost story. Set in
1836, after the era of the French Colonial rule, Gardley unearths
the history of Louisiana's free women of colour and illustrates
how these women gained their freedom and prosperity, through
living a life of 'sex, lies and sand'.

The action takes place after the death of Lazare Albans, a white
French grandee, and centres on his mistress, Beartrice Albans,
their three unwed children and house servant Makeda. The death
of Lazare has costly implications and the family are forced to
consider their future. Beartrice is a formidable matriarch of
the family and has become one of the city's wealthiest women
through a life of *plaçage* – a financial system whereby mixed-race
mistresses and common-law wives, and their mixed children,
could negotiate for and be willed freedom, property, money and
education.

Beartrice is determined to maintain her house, quality of life and
freedom without surrendering her children to the life of a *placeé*.
However, her strong-minded, sexually charged eldest daughter

Agnès, described in the play as 'the color of butter', has her eye on the wealthy Rámon Le Pip, after a flirtatious encounter at church which resulted in him secretly slipping her a love note written on a church hymnal requesting her presence at the masked ball, which she concealed between her breasts. Despite being banned from the ball by her mother, Agnès is determined to attend in the hope of becoming Rámon Le Pip's mistress. There is only one problem: mothers are required to attend the masked balls to negotiate the price and sign her papers for their offspring. Knowing that she will not able to become his mistress without her mother's consent, Agnès singlehandedly devises a plan. She convinces her youngest and darkest-complexioned sibling, Odette, to sneak out of the house and attend the ball disguised as Beartrice to negotiate and sign her papers. Odette reluctantly agrees to escort her sister to the ball for the chance to meet men and on the promise that, if caught, Agnès will take full responsibility. Agnès applies extra padding and a mask to Odette to complete the transformation. But when they get to the ball, things do not go as Agnès planned.

Summary (extract)

Agnès (pronounced 'An-yes') (nineteen, eldest daughter, sensual) and Odette are on the porch of their house after attending the masked ball. **Odette** looks radiantly beautiful as her long hair flows freely and the extra padding which masked her beautiful figure has gone. Her beauty was not lost on **Rámon Le Pip**, or the other gentlemen at the ball, much to the irritation of her elder sister. **Agnès** prides herself on her lighter complexion and beautiful body and initially saw no competition in her darker-skinned younger sister, but is now forced to see **Odette**'s beauty as her rival.

Agnès Look at you! Looking like you were born downwind of an outhouse. Ankles exposed like you just come from a womb, breasts sitting out like they holding court, but everyone know they guilty, hair falling off your shoulders like you never brushed up against a comb, and I be damed as the devil if that rouge on your lips is not blood you bit free just so your kiss could kill. You look a whore, Odette. You look like something even a mother couldn't love. Walking round the ball like it's your planet and the rest of us is renting a room. I turned my back on you once when I looked up and you were waltzing with every Harry, Dick and Little Pete from Salkehatchie to Suwannee. Like a trollop. Like a jack-legged Jezabelle. I was so mad I could have ate my face! You were supposed to be acting like you were *maman*. You were supposed to be sitting in the balcony with the other mothers sipping gossip and talking tea. I had to hunt you down twice to get my papers signed and when you finally met Rámon, you took all night, batting your eyes and smiling your teeth so bright you'd think the lights went out. This was supposed to be my night but you couldn't even stay in costume. You told yourself you were the belle of the ball and you went to town shaking your hips and swinging that tongue, and now I just want to ring your scrawny little neck. […] Upset?! Upset is a kitten caught up a tree! I'm a big cat and I got my claws *out*! […] What I care about waking up *Maman*? I hope she do wake, I hope she come down swinging her cane so I can tell her how whorish you been and maybe she can knock some sense into you. I've never been so embarrassed in all my nineteen years.

From

MELODY LOSES HER MOJO

by Keith Saha

Melody Loses Her Mojo received a world premiere at the Playhouse, Liverpool, on 20 September 2013, in a co-production between 20 Stories High, Liverpool Everyman and Playhouse and the Curve, Leicester. This production was written and directed by Co-Artistic Director of 20 Stories High, Keith Saha, and performed by Remmie Milner (Melody), Darren Kuppan (Rizia), Simone James (Blessing), Samuel Dutton (Puppeteer/Jeff), Zoë Hunter (Puppeteer/Jackie), Hobbit (Musician/Beatboxer) and Hannah Marshall (Musician/Cellist).

Keith Saha combines actors, puppeteers, dancers, musicians and visual artists to create a refreshingly innovative and unique piece of hip-hop theatre for young audiences. Drawing on his own childhood in a care home and inspired by the stories from young people around the country, Keith Saha uses real-life experiences to write a play which presents the current issues faced by young people in care. The play highlights the inadequacies of the care system which results in young people to be separated from their siblings, communities and countries. In the care home, overworked social workers are likely to suffer from mental breakdowns leaving young care leavers without a support network to help them transition to the next stage of their lives.

With a drug-addicted mother, fifteen-year-old Melody was placed in care when she was just ten along with her six-year-old sister Harmony. The sisters were placed together in a long-term foster home, taking them far away from their community to a farm in the middle of nowhere. But not long after being placed, Melody was assigned back to the care home alone, as foster mothers Claire and Hazel came to the conclusion that she was 'too much to handle'. Before the siblings were separated, Harmony gave Melody her Mojo – a toy monster which is also a rucksack. Through what the playwright describes as 'magical realism', the Mojo comes to life, displaying the psychological states of Melody. The art of puppetry is applied to transform the Mojo/rucksack into many different characters and creatures which help to keep Melody on the right path.

Five years later, Melody has lived in fourteen different homes. Without any adult guidance or family, Melody lives a life of drugs, fighting and numerous encounters with the police. Despite her trust issues she is able to build a strong friendship with Rizla. This relationship is threatened when the new arrival at the care home, Blessing, from Nigeria, wins Rizla's attention. Melody's demons resurface.

Unlike her sister, Harmony has stayed with the same foster parents and flourished into a confident, horse-riding young woman. A week before Harmony's birthday, Melody receives the news that Harmony's foster parents have started the adoption process. With fears of losing her little sister forever, Melody is determined to hold on to the only family she knows.

Summary (extract)

Fifteen-year-old **Melody** is mixed race (African and white) and dresses like a tomboy: slicked-back hair, red trainers, tracksuit bottoms, and an oversized hoody with a big pair of hooped ear-rings. After receiving news that her residential worker, Jeff, is leaving and is therefore unable to take her to **Harmony**'s birthday in a week's time, **Melody** has decided to take matters into her own hands. **Melody**, **Rizla** and **Blessing** all have reasons to escape from the care home. **Melody** directs the group to camp near **Harmony**'s home. Leaving **Rizla** and **Blessing** at the camp, Melody knocks on the door of **Harmony**'s house and convinces **Harmony** to play a game of hide and seek in an attempt to get **Harmony** out of the house. But when **Melody** returns to the camp with **Harmony**, **Rizla** persuades her to take **Harmony** back. They all arrive at the bottom of **Harmony**'s street. **Melody** is faced with the hardest decision.

Melody   OK, sweetheart … In a minute you are going to be a
big brave girl for me and go and knock on the big red door … You
know which house you live in, don't you?

Harmony *nods.*

See … that's because you are such a clever girl. You're a lot
cleverer than me … do you know that?

Harmony *shakes her head.*

Well you are … I'm sorry if you were scared before … I just got a
bit upset … but I'm OK now … are we OK? …

Harmony *nods.*

… Good … Because you know I love you loads, don't you? (*She
nods*) … And although I want to be with you all the time … I
can't … and the best place for you to be is with Mummy Hazel
and Mummy Clare because they love you soooo much … just as
much as I do. And do you know what? I might not see you very
much over the next few years but that's OK because we won't
forget each other, and we'll have the rest of our lives to get to
know each other better, won't we? Because I'm your big sister and
big sisters never go away … I'll always be here to back you up …
when you need back up … or if you need me to beat any boys up.

Harmony *gives* **Mojo** *back to* **Melody**.

Are you giving him back to me? Do you think I can look after him
properly this time? (*She nods*) … I will, you know … I'll fix him
up … and I will look after him. OK? Good.

Melody *and* **Harmony** *hug.*

Go on, then … Bye bye … love you loads.

Harmony *walks up to her door* …

Go on sweetheart.

Harmony *exits.*

From

BULRUSHER

by Eisa Davis

Pulitzer finalist, *Bulrusher* received its world premiere at Urban Stages/Playwrights' Preview Productions in New York in March 2006. It was directed by Leah C. Gardiner with the following cast: Zabryna Guevara/Donna Duplantier (Bulrusher), Tinashe Kajese (Vera), Charlotte Colavin (Madame), Guiesseppe Jones (Logger), Robert Beitzel (Boy) and Peter Bradbury/Darrill Rosen (Schoolch).

Eisa Davis is the niece of political activist Angela Davis and an exceptional woman in her own right, with several accolades for her artistic contributions to theatre. Playwright, singer, composer and actor, there is simply nothing that is unattainable for this formidable woman. *Bulrusher* is a great example of her fearlessness when adopting lyrical language to pose difficult questions. The play boldly and unapologetically embraces the Boontling language, a pidgin dialect invented and spoken only in Boonville, Northern California. This jargon language was designed by the residents to isolate and confuse those who were not privy to over 1,300 words featured in the Boontling dictionary and to unify residents, enabling them to have private conversations in public places about taboo subject matters.

The play is set in Boonville, California, a small town in the Anderson Valley of Mendocino County, north of San Francisco, in 1955. The year is significant for Emmett Till, a fourteen-year-old African American boy who was murdered in Mississippi for flirting with a white girl. Although the play takes place at the early beginnings of the Civil Rights movement in the north, Eisa Davis deliberately sets the action thousands of miles away, in an area where the black female protagonist, Bulrusher, is one of the only African American residents. Bulrusher is being pursued by a young white character called 'Boy', who is adamant to have her as his girlfriend. This essentially heightens the themes depicted in the play of racial inequalities, humanity, love and innocence.

The play focuses on Bulrusher – as implied by her name, an
orphan, illegitimate child. As an infant Bulrusher was placed in
a basket and sent floating down the Navarro river, later rescued
and raised by a near-silent teacher Schoolch. Bulrusher's early
encounters with the Navarro river have a long-term effect on her,
as she is anointed with the 'gift' of being a clairvoyant – able
to read a person's past and future by simply touching the same
water they have immersed themselves in. Although she is able
to see into the future and past of others, she is unable to read her
own life to discover the identity of her parents. Segregated from
anyone who looks like her, on the arrival of a black Southern
American woman, Vera, Bulrusher is able for the first time to see
and fall in love with the image of herself.

At the very heart of this play is a black woman's journey to
self-love. Eisa Davis calls out to black women everywhere,
inviting them to learn, embrace and fall in love with who they are.

Summary (extract)

This speech takes place near the end of the play. Eighteen-year-old
Bulrusher has fallen in love with **Vera**, the first African American
woman she has ever met. But **Madame** has succeeded in tearing
them apart. Through **Madame**'s attempts to separate the two
girls, **Bulrusher** has discovered that **Madame** (owner of the local
brothel) is her mother, the woman responsible for placing her in
the basket and sending her down the Navarro river, and **Vera** is
her relative. **Bulrusher** seeks solace at the Navarro river, where
she is confronted by her mother for the second time in her life –
only this time she wants answers and an apology.

Bulrusher   Yes I can. Yes I can. I remember floating in the night, the fog and the coyotes – didn't know what that sound was then but I do now. Mr Jeans found me at Barney Flats, but I was there for days. I begged to be found. I talked to the sun with my fingers, kept closing my fist around it every time it went down trying to keep it with me. But the night would always come. And the river was so thin there, deep as a teardrop – but I kept myself alive. Why? To find you? To lose the only one who ever really touched me? Schoolch never did, he doesn't know how. Only told me to sit up straight. Vera touched me, gave me softness and you made her leave. You knew she was going when I saw her last, didn't you. (**Madame** *is silent*). Of course you did. So is she gonna kill the baby or be the preacher's wife who got raped by a cop? […] I'm not angry. I'm gonna kill you. I want to kill something. Walk toward the edge of that bluff. Do it.

Madame *doesn't move and* **Bulrusher** *aims her shotgun.*

Back to me. Go to the ocean and look at it.

Madame *walks to the edge of the cliff.*

See it gnashing its teeth? It wants you. Didn't want me. But it still wants to eat. Salt gonna sting your eyes, gonna burn you. All that seaweed down there is gonna grab you and drown you.

[…]

You already dead, ever since you tried to kill me. You been dead.

[…]

Dead for money. Wanted some damn money steada me. Well go get it. I threw it in there for you. Its all yours.

From

RUINED

by Lynn Nottage

Ruined is a Pulitzer Prize-winning play by Lynn Nottage. The
play was originally commissioned by and received its world
premiere at the Goodman Theatre, Chicago in November 2008,
in a co-production with Manhattan Theatre Club directed by Kate
Whoriskey. This was followed by a run in New York at Manhattan
Theatre Club in February 2009. It received its European premiere
at the Almeida Theatre, London, in April 2010. The London
production was directed by Indhu Rubasingham and starred
Michelle Asante (Salima), Jenny Jules (Mama Nadi), Pippa
Bennett-Warner (Sophie), Kehinde Fadipe (Josephine), Lucian
Msamati (Christian), Silas Carson (Mr Harari), Okezie Morro
(Jerome Kisembe), Steve Toussaint (Commander Osembenga),
David Ajala (Fortune), Damola Adelaja (Simon) and Joel Kangudi
(Soldier/Laurent).

Exasperated by the lack of media attention given to what is
known as the 'deadliest conflict worldwide since World War II',
Lynn Nottage's powerful play *Ruined* brings awareness of the
continuing conflict in the Democratic Republic of Congo, a war
which has resulted in over 5.4 million deaths. Motivated by the
desire to give a voice to the unseen African women in war-torn
Congo, Nottage travelled to East Africa, conducting extensive
interviews with Congolese women who shared their painful
experiences of being subjected to life-threatening sexual violence
and torture inflicted by rebel soldiers and government militias.
These real-life experiences have informed the characters depicted
in the play. *Ruined* is a mouthpiece for the unheard African
women of Congo who struggle to survive the war imposed on
their bodies. Lynn Nottage depicts the women in her play not as
victims but as survivors, resilient and strong.

The play takes place in Mama Nadi's bar, located in a small
mining town deep in the Democratic Republic of Congo. We
quickly realise that Mama Nadi's business extends beyond selling

alcoholic beverages, food and cigarettes, when travelling salesman Christian presents her with three teenage girls who are willing to work in her brothel. Mama agrees to pay $20 for Sophie, a young, attractive girl with an air of defiance. Christian heavily persuades Mama to take at no extra charge Salima, a sturdy peasant girl whose face betrays world-weariness. Mama reluctantly agrees when provided with chocolate that reminds her of her past.

Both Sophie and Salima carry the physical and psychological traumas of their past. Sophie is simply described as 'ruined' and finds the act of walking painfully difficult. Salima has been gang-raped for five months by rebel soldiers and as a result is pregnant. They both have been deemed dishonourable by their families and as a result can no longer return to their homes.

Within the walls of her own establishment Mama Nadi sets the rules: no politics, no fighting and no guns. What Mama says, goes. Mama Nadi has made a lucrative business by offering a place of refuge for ruined girls and for the soldiers, miners and rebels a neutral ground where they can purchase drinks, food and sex. But with the civil war just outside her door, it's not long before the conflict starts seeping into her establishment.

Summary (extract)

Nineteen-year-old **Salima** is from the Hama tribe. She was captured and gang-raped by the rebel soldiers for five months and consequently ostracised from her small village and torn apart from her husband **Fortune** and child **Beatrice**. She has now found refuge at **Mama**'s bar-cum-brothel. But things take a sudden turn when **Fortune** arrives looking for her. **Salima** is pregnant and, to the confusion of her only friend **Sophie**, refuses to see him. **Mama** has her own reasons for keeping them apart and has done her best to shield **Fortune** from seeing **Salima**, but with her husband camped outside the establishment for the last two days in the rain, **Salima** is forced to defend her decision to stay hidden to **Sophie**.

Salima   Stupid man. Why did he have to come?

He called me a filthy dog, and said I tempted them. Why else would it happen? Five months in the bush, passed between the soldiers like a wash rag. Used. I was made poison by their fingers, that is what he said. He had no choice but to turn away from me, because I dishonoured him.

Why are you defending him? Then you go with him! Do you know what I was doing on that morning? (*A calm washes over her.*) I was working in our garden, picking the last of the sweet tomatoes. I put Beatrice down in the shade of a frangipani tree, because my back was giving me some trouble. Forgiven? Where was fortune? He was in town fetching a new iron pot. "Go," I said. "Go, today man, or you won't have dinner tonight!" I had been after him for a new pot for a month. And finally on that day the damn man had to go and get it. A new pot. The sun was about to crest, but I had to put in another hour before it got too hot. It was such a clear and open sky. This splendid bird, a peacock, had come into the garden to taunt me, and was showing off its feathers. I stooped down and called to the bird: "Wssht, Wssht." And I felt a shadow cut across my back, and when I stood four men were there over me, smiling, wicked schoolboy smiles. "Yes?" I said. And the tall soldier slammed the butt of his gun into my cheek. Just like that. It was so quick, I didn't even know I'd fallen to the ground. Where did they come from? How could I not have heard them? One of the soldiers held me down with his foot. He was so heavy, thick like an ox and his boot was cracked and weathered like it had been left out in the rain for weeks. His boot was pressing my chest and the cracks in the leather had the look of drying sorghum. His foot was so heavy, and it was all I could see as the others … "took" me. My baby was crying. She was a good baby. Beatrice never cried, but she was crying, screaming. "Shhh," I said. "Shhh." And right then … (*Closes her eyes.*) A soldier stomped on her head with his boot. And she was quiet. (A moment. Salima releases:) Where was everybody? WHERE WAS EVERYBODY?! I fought them! I did! But they still took me from my home. They took me through the bush – raiding thieves. Fucking demons! "She is for everyone, soup to be had before dinner," that is what someone said. They tied me to a tree by my foot, and the men came whenever they wanted soup. I make fires, I cook food, I listen to their stupid songs, I carry bullets, I clean wounds, I wash blood from their clothing, and, and, and … I lay there as they tore me to pieces, until I was raw … five months. Five months. Chained like a goat. These men fighting … fighting for our liberation. Still I close my eyes and I see such terrible things. Things I cannot stand to have in my head. How can men be this way?

(*A moment.*)

It was such a clear and open sky. So, so beautiful. How could I not hear them coming?

A peacock wandered into my garden, and the tomatoes were ripe beyond belief. Our fields of red sorghum were so perfect, it was going to be a fine season. Fortune thought so, too, and we could finally think about planning a trip on the ferry to visit his brother. Oh God, please give me back that morning. "Forget the pot, Fortune. Stay …" "Stay," that's what I would tell him. What did I do, Sophie? I must have done something. How did I get in the middle of their fight?

It isn't his baby. It's the child of a monster, and there's no telling what it will be. Now, he's willing to forgive me, and is it that simple, Sophie? But what happens when the baby is born, will he be able to forgive the child, will I? And, and … and even if I do, I don't think I'll be able to forgive him.

I walked into the family compound expecting wide open arms. An embrace. Five months, suffering. I suffered every single second of it. And my family gave me the back of their heads. And he, the man I loved since I was fourteen, chased me away with a green switch. He beat my ankles raw. And I dishonoured him? I dishonoured him?! Where was he? Buying a pot? He was too proud to bear my shame … but not proud enough to protect me from it. Let him sit in the rain.

From

IN THE CONTINUUM

by Danai Gurira and Nikkole Salter

In the Continuum received its world premiere at Primary Stages in New York City in September 2005. It subsequently moved to the Perry Street Theatre in November 2005, where it was produced by Primary Stages in association with Perry Street Theatre. The production was directed by Robert O'Hara with the following cast: Nikkole Salter (Nia and others), Danai Gurira (Abigail and others), Tinasha Kajese and Antu Jacob (Understudies). The original production received an international tour from April 2006 through August 2007.

In the Continuum was developed in the third year of a graduate school acting project at New York University (NYU) and successfully grew into a professional international touring production. Selected as one of the best ten plays of the year by the *New York Times*, it tells the story of two black women infected with the HIV virus. The writers, who also perform in the play, wrote *In the Continuum* in response to contemporary HIV/AIDS statistics which alarmingly suggested that black females represented the highest rate of new infection both in the USA and Africa.

This two-hander takes place in two different parts of the world: Nia is a teenage African American girl who lives in South Central, Los Angles, and Abigail is a newsreader living in Harare, Zimbabwe. The girls never meet but are connected through the shared experience of discovering that the men in their lives have infected them with HIV. As they narrate their personal journeys, their stories smoothly transition from running in parallel to brief moments of interweaving. We are forced to recognize that HIV fails to discriminate between those who get infected with the disease – the virus spreads irrespective of social position, economics or age. In spite of the subject matter, Salter and Gurira bring humanity to the story which is moving, heart-breaking and in parts quite funny.

The characters are polar opposites. Nia lacks drive, passion and direction; she rarely attends school and was recently fired from Nordstrom for taking a five-finger discount one time too many. She generally drifts through life, living vicariously through her boyfriend Darnell, a talented, handsome and popular basketball player with a real potential to be a star. Nia dreams of a celebrity lifestyle and sees Darnell as her lottery ticket to obtaining materialistic success. Abigail, in contrast, is a middle-class, career-driven wife, pregnant with her second child and having marital problems. She has dreams of climbing the career ladder from newsreader for the Zimbabwe Broadcasting Corp to working for CNN.

In the Continuum chronicles the personal journeys of both women, from denial through isolation to self-discovery, playing multiple characters to depict some of the cultural and social attitudes that are present in today's world.

Summary (extract)

Teenager **Nia** has discovered that she is HIV positive and pregnant with **Darnell**'s baby. **Gail** (**Darnell**'s mother) has confessed that she knew about **Darnell**'s medical history but decided to keep it a 'private family matter' to protect her son's reputation. Fearful that **Nia** will expose her son and potentially damage his career, **Gail** has given **Nia** a cheque for $5,000 to remain silent.

Nia   It smell like booty. I wish I could fly away. Dirty ass motel.
Guess what, baby. Guess what? (*Dumping her purse.*) Today
your mommy opened her purse to see how much money she
had and she had a five dollar bill and a $5,000 check. $5,000.
(*Folding up the check and putting it aside.*) But you know what?
We don't need his money. No, we don't! 'Cause mommy will go
tomorrow and see if they still want her at Nordstom. What was
they talkin' 'bout payin'? Five dollars. But no, baby, no, we can
do it. We just got to budget. (*Tearing a piece of the five dollar
bill with each item.*) See this, this right here is for my retirement
fund. 'Cause Oprah says you should pay yourself first. This, this
is for your college fund, 'cause you going to college. This is for
rent … on our mansion in Malibu. And my Mercedes. What else?
What else you want, baby? You can have anything you want.
Oh wait! (*Tearing the last piece in three.*) Gas, water, and lights.
What! That' the life right there, baby. You got retirement, college,
mansion, Mercedes, gas, water, lights. What! Ooooo! Mommy
forgot to put food in the budget? How mommy forgot to put food
in the budget? But there's no more money. There's $5,000. (*She
breaks down in tears.*) Because he knew. He knew the whole time
– and he knows you're his baby cuz he the one made me pregnant.
And now she thinks she can just throw $5,000 at me and I'ma just
be quiet? $5,000 dollars. I sold myself for $5,000. Nope, baby,
that's how much I cost. That's how much you cost. (*Balling up the
check and throwing it down.*) No, no, we don't need his money.
This is what we gonna do. (*Picking up the pieces of the five dollar
bill.*) I'ma take the light money and make it the food money. Cuz
we gotta eat. But we don't need no lights. (*A la 'The Roof is on
Fire'.*) We don't need no lights let the muthafuckas burn! (*She
b-boxes and makes a beat on the furniture.*) Come on, baby. Cuz
we got, huh? What we got, huh? What we got?!

(*Periodically breaking down and breaking rhythm.*)

We got, we got Sunlight, Insight, Out of sight – out of mind.
Full-time, Lifetime
Out-of-time
I'm outta my mind
We gon' Re-define

Discipline
Undermine that bottom line

(*Applying perfume.*)

Drench myself in Vaseline
Make myself look feminine
I'll be dressed and drapped in Calvin Klein.
And he'll come home at dinnertime.
My womb is free of guilt and grime.
Before this change, before this crime.
Before the fall, before the climb. (*She begins to pray.*)
Please keep me from this constant grind
Help me see, although I'm blind
Help me breathe despite the slime
Help me live if you're inclined
Please don't decline my prayer.
I know it's nobody's fault but mine
I won't bitch, complain or whine
If you help me out, one more time
I will not let you down.
I'll give up sex, weed and wine.
Everything. Everything.
Just plant my feet on solid ground.

(*She sobs.*) No. No! This what we gon' do. (*Picks up the check.*)
Tomorrow we're going to go to that scholarship ceremony. And
I'm gonna make Darnell look me in the face and tell me I'm only
worth $5,000. Then, I'm going to stand there in front of all those
recruiters, in front of the whole world and I'ma just say it. And
then all the girls he been with's gon' know. And all the girls he
was thinking about doin's gon' know. And then everybody will
know. (*Balling the check up and throwing it down again.*) I'm
worth more than this money. (*She begins to exit. She doubles back
for the check.*) Tomorrow.

From

MY NAME IS ...

by Sudha Bhuchar

My Name is ... was produced by Tamasha Theatre Company and premiered at the Arcola Theatre, London in April 2014, followed by performances at the Tron Theatre, Glasgow, before receiving a UK national tour September–October 2014. The play was directed by Philip Osment with the following cast: Kiran Sonia Sawar (Ghazala/Gaby), Umar Ahmed (Farhan) and Karen Bartke (Suzy/Sajida).

Sudha Bhuchar's play was inspired by the 2006 headlines which covered the story of twelve-year-old mixed-race (Asian/white) Molly Campbell, who disappeared from Shetland and was later discovered living with her father in Pakistan. Several media reports falsely incriminated Molly's Pakistani father, suggesting that he was a Jihadi fundamentalist who kidnapped his daughter for an arranged marriage. It later emerged that Molly fled on her own accord and the media story was silenced.

My Name is ... is a verbatim play which reveals the true events that led a young (Pakistani/white) girl to leave her hometown of Glasgow and go to live in Pakistan with her father. Sudha Bhuchar conducted interviews with the father, mother and child in question and from these interviews presents a story which illustrates modern British attitudes towards Islamic faith, cultural practices and interracial relationships.

For the purpose of the play, the characters' names differ from their real ones. The action takes place two years after the story was reported in the press, with daughter Ghazala, now fourteen years old, still living in Pakistan with her father, Farhan. The story playfully jumps back and forth through different timespans of the characters' lives as they recount their reactions to the press, details of the parents' marriage and encounters with members of their community, family and friends which influenced negatively on their relationship. The narrative of this three-dimensional story collides, overlaps, contradicts and interweaves to illustrate the complexities of their cross-cultural relationship and the impact it had on their four children.

Suzy and Farhan's love affair began in Glasgow in the 1980s. Their fun, carefree relationship quickly blossoms into marriage. Suzy willingly agrees to convert to Muslim for marriage, initially to appease Farhan and his mother. Her interest in the Muslim religion grows and she completely and freely immerses herself in Islamic culture: reading the Koran, cooking Asian food for the community, changing her name to Sajida and wearing the niqab. Suzy and Farhan have four children who are given Islamic names and raised to practise the Muslim religion. Although Suzy's dedication to the Muslim religion has a positive effect on Farhan, who becomes a 'proper good Muslim man', her efforts fail to meet the expectations of her mother-in-law, who unapologetically chastizes her failings at any given opportunity. Dressed in the niqab, Suzy encounters daily abuse from members of her community. As the demographics of the Asian population increases in Glasgow, the abuse on Asian people worsens, resulting in young people forming gangs to protect themselves. Suzy decides to move the family to Blackburn, but Farhan's job in Glasgow means the family are forced to separate during weekdays. The pressures of living a Muslim life, together with the constant abuse and criticism from her community, mother-in-law and husband, has begun to take a toll on Suzy, causing her to renounce the Muslim faith and have a nervous breakdown. She is considered an unfit mother and Farhan is given full custody of the children. The couple separate. The children live with Farhan and his new wife in Pakistan, with the condition of Suzy seeing the children once a year.

When the children visit for the second time, Suzy pleads with them to extend their stay. But with all four children living with their mum, her new boyfriend and his two dogs in a one-bedroom flat, and with Suzy's changed lifestyle, things rapidly take a turn for the worse.

Summary (extract)

Ghazala (fourteen, Scottish Pakistani) and her siblings have reluctantly succumbed to their mum's suicidal plea for her children to stay longer with her during their second visit since the separation. The one-bedroom flat is over-capacity with **Suzy** and her non-Muslim boyfriend **Lenny**, the four children and two dogs. During her stay **Ghazala** quickly realizes that her mum has adopted a new lifestyle, steering away from a Muslim way of life with the expectation that her children will follow suit. In the extract, **Ghazala** narrates how her siblings are not prepared to give up the Islamic way of life without a fight.

Ghazala   Mama's boyfriend … Lenny … He came and he had two dogs …

(*To* **Sana** *who is off.*) Sana. No! Nahin Karo.

… it was all dog hairs and cobwebs and the cobwebs were stuck with hair … we had to sleep on the living-room floor and it was only a one-bedroom flat and it was four kids, and mama and Lenny and two dogs … Mama used to tell my brothers to go to the pubs and send Lenny with them. They used to go play snooker, and drink sharab […]

I remember I had a birthday party … My eleventh … Lenny was a wicked cook. Wicked. Zabardast! He made my birthday cake. Chocolate sponge with chocolate icing and then cream, then chocolate sponge with chocolate icing and then cream, and then chocolate sponge with chocolate icing and then cream … I was a kid, man … and if you get a kid and you say, 'what do you want the most?' (*Answering.*) 'Chocolate cake.' That's what strangers do. They give kids candy and they kidnap them don't they? Give candy and the kids are under your spell but, em … (*Suddenly stopping herself.*) I talk too much and you're recording it like. I talk too much …

Mama what she did, she took all our shalwar kameezes. All our full sleeves, full length trousers, T-shirts. She put it all in a black bin bag and gave it to the charity shop, and got some money. She went and got little short skirts, sleeveless T-shirts, backless T-shirts and tight trousers, and we were like …

[…]

'Oh wha …' like we didn't know what to say.

Omar bhai was like … that's it. 'I'm not gonna live here. I won't let you be like this.' Like to my little sisters. He had a massive fight with Lenny. So Lenny kicked him out. Mama just sat there … just watched some other guy kick out her son out of her house.

[…]

And then … only Zain bhai and me were left. So a couple of

months later, what happened ke. Zain bhai, he kept on getting some parcels and letters from London. There was … it had the money in it. Finally Zain bhai … usney jama kar kar ke karke karkey, he saved up the amount … and … (*She gets upset.*)

[…]

After that I was proper upset. Oh my God! That's everyone gone now. Mama she … she went everywhere I went. She dropped me off to school. She'd be standing five minutes before break at the school fence. I came back from school one day and Lenny and Mama they were … You know how when you get that disappointed face on you? They had that face.

They are back in the scene

What happened?

[…] I got changed and I came down and they said …

They pulled out this map and they showed …

[…]

I didn't quite understand … We left and we travelled all through the night in a wee small car … a wee small Suzuki car …

From

CHILD OF THE DIVIDE

by Sudha Bhuchar

Child of the Divide was co-produced by Tamasha Theatre
Company and Polka Theatre Company and received its world
premiere at Polka Theatre, London on 5 May 2006. This
production was directed by the former Artistic Director of
Tamasha Theatre Company, Kristine Landon-Smith, with the
following cast: Tony Jayawardena (Buttameez/Manohar Lal),
Rina Fatania (Hasina/Zainab), Divian Ladwa (Pali/Altaaf), Krupa
Pattani (Aisha/Kaushalya) and Amit Sharma (Pagal Head/Shakur).

Adapted from the short story *Pali* by Bhisham Sahni, *Child
of the Divide* by Sudha Bhuchar is a gripping and tragic story
about love, loss and belonging. The action takes place during the
most traumatic time in Indian history: the partition of India and
newly formed Pakistan, an event which led to a brutal massacre.
Told through the perspective of a Hindu child named Pali who
is separated from his father at the border crossing during the
partition, Bhuchar's play conveys the physical, psychological and
emotional trauma, as well as the fears of the Hindu community.

A slip of the hand separates Pali from his father, leaving Pali
without a family or a home in a country where his life is in
danger. Muslim couple Zainab and Shakur, unable to conceive,
yearn to have a child of their own. When they find Pali, they
believe that faith has brought him into their lives and adopt him,
changing his name and faith to mask his Hindu identity. But what
starts out as an act of kindness quickly transpires into something
more profound.

Pali (now Altaaf) is allowed to play with the refugee children at
the camp, with new friends Hasina, who is also a love-interest,
and Aisha. It is not long before they are confronted by local bully
Pagal Head and with his sidekick, who is also Hasina and Aisha's
friend Buttameez. While the group are playing near Pali's former
family home, he speaks about his home and the truth about his
real identity is discovered by Pagal Head, who threatens to inform

his dad, a dangerous man who goes around killing Hindus. This revelation triggers Hasina to open up about her Pakistani-Hindu dual identity and the abuse she experienced from both sides. Pali realizes that he is not the only one living a lie.

Seven years later, his father returns to reunite Pali with his birth mother, who has mourned his loss since the day they parted. Pali must decide whether to leave the world he has now fully adjusted to or return to a new land with his biological family.

Summary (extract)

Hasina (a child who lives at the refugee camp) is with **Pali** and **Aisha** a while after the fight between the local bully **Pagal Head** and **Buttameez** against **Pali**. **Hasina** wipes **Pali**'s bruises as they talk about the fight, **Buttameez**, and their latest discovery about **Pali**'s real identity. But **Hasina** also has a secret to reveal.

Hasina I think about my ammi all the time, and I know she thinks about me. […] She thinks I'm safe with my uncle. […] Can I tell you a secret?

I'm half-half so I got two names. Hasina 'cos my abu said I was his beautiful princess, and Sita which was my secret with my mama. […] Sita stayed pure, but like no one believed her and in the end she asked Mother Earth to take her back.

[…]

Mama and Sita was too good for this world. But I'm bad. My uncle said that my abu died because of me. […] Hindus killed him 'cos he married a Hindu and they don't like that. Bloods shouldn't mix. But mine is.

[…]

Because of my Muslim blood, my mama sent me with my uncle to be safe here in Pakistan. Because of my Hindu blood, my uncle left me by the side of the road. Sitting on a stone … alone. He said he couldn't love me because in my face he could see the Hindus that killed his brother. I didn't want my abba to die … *Allah ki kasam* … I loved him. He made me and my mama pretty things and – (*Looking at her battered shoes.*) – decorated my shoes with taré and sequins. A soft lady found me. She took my hand and brought me to the camp across the border. I came with other lost children like Buttameez.

[…]

You're lucky your new mum loves you. She's always calling you in to eat a sweet rusk or khatai.

[…]

My amma will come and get me.

[…]

I post her a letter every day.

From

ALASKA

by DC Moore

Alaska premiered at the Royal Court Jerwood Theatre Upstairs,
London in May 2007, directed by Maria Aberg with the following
cast: Fiona Wade (Mamta), Christine Bottomley (Emma),
Sebastian Armesto (Adam), Harry Hepple (Russell), Thomas
Morrison (Chris) and Rafe Spall (Frank). DC Moore is a graduate
of the Royal Court Young Writers' Programme and *Alaska* was his
first play.

Frank is a racist, loner, bible-reading university dropout who
makes a living from dealing cannabis to students from his old
university and working at the multiplex cinema. At the cinema,
Frank is the sex magnet of the retail establishment with an
on-going fling with worker Emma, as well as other admirers. His
life is completely shaken up when Mamta, a young outspoken
Asian woman, is employed as the kiosk supervisor. Similar to
Emma, Mamta is sexually attracted to Frank and finds a moment
to hit on him. Despite nearly succumbing to Mamta's sexual
advances, Frank is keen to stay committed to his racist attitudes.
Frank wins the affection and sympathy from the ladies in the
establishments when they discover that the anniversary of his
father's death is soon approaching. Emma quickly defends his
flickered moments of racial gags and insults, attributing them
to his loss. But when Mamta is forced to reprimand Frank for
smoking on the job in front of customers, Frank loses the battle to
suppress his extreme racist beliefs. However, he is no competition
for intellectually savvy Mamta, who quickly puts Frank in his
place. Unsatisfied with being verbally slapped by Mamta, Frank
takes his revenge, resulting in a physical altercation with her
brother which in turn becomes Frank's biggest wake-up call.
Frank's life spirals out of control and the real Frank is revealed.

This is a play about revenge, lies and racism.

Summary (extract)

Mamta (nineteen years old) spots **Frank** sitting on the steps
of a church, looking troubled. She is convinced that his mood
is a result of the anniversary of his father's death the previous
day. She attempts to console him. **Frank** snaps. He unearths his
deep-rooted racial hatred in a long and unapologetic rant based on
ignorance, senseless interpretations of the Bible and white-power
ideologies. Straight-talking **Mamta** waits for **Frank** to run out of
steam before giving him a few well-founded home truths.

Mamta   Are you done?

Frank nods

You know. I hope. (*Referring to the church.*) If your God is in there, I really hope He can hear you. All this.

[...]

I mean. Does talking like that, all that, speaking like this to me, does that give you a boner/or –?

[...]

Charming. Really. I can see why Emma went for you. Or was it cos she was too drunk to stand up?

[...]

I fucking am [funny]. What's black and eats bananas? Half of London. What do you call a dead Paki? A good start. Don't be thinking you can shock me, alright? Or push me around. Fucking … lecture me. You know the funny thing is, you actually sound a bit like my dad. He was always saying stuff like that. Like, doesn't matter who I marry as long as they're not either black or Muslim and he'll rant on about everything that happened back in Uganda. So actually as well as being wrong, you're also being. Very. Deeply. Unoriginal. (*Pause.*) But I think, I think some people need to keep talking like you do. Cos if they stopped they'd realise that, God, I've got. Nothing. The only way I can function is by directing all this shit out at other people. Because if I stopped. If I stopped doing it for one second and looked at my life. And was truly honest with myself, I'd have to take the nearest knife and stab myself in the heart. (*Pause.*) And. And d'ya know what's really funny?

[...]

Having listened to you now, I do think Emma was genuinely mad for letting you and your tiny white cock anywhere near her.

Pausing briefly for effect, **Mamta** *picks up her shopping and exits.*

From

FISH EYES

by Anita Majumdar

Fish Eyes premiered at the Belfry SPARK Festival in 2012, choreographed and performed by Anita Majumdar and originally directed by Gregory Prest. In October 2014, Brian Quirt directed a Cultch and PuSh Performing Arts Festival presentation of a Nightswimming production which opened at the Great Canadian Theatre. The play subsequently toured across Canada and internationally for eight years to much acclaim and has toured to high schools as part of 'Kids' Helpline' and the '411 Initiative Tour Program' to raise self-esteem in young teenage girls.

Fish Eyes is the first part of a trilogy (also including *Boys With Cars* and *Let Me Borrow That Top*) by the multitalented artist Anita Majumdar. *The Fish Eyes Trilogy* is a series of coming-of-age stories about three teenage girls. In *Fish Eyes*, Mujamdar combines storytelling and traditional Indian dance to tell the moving story of seventeen-year-old Indo-Canadian girl Meena. This one-woman play is packed with funny dialogue, with Bollywood star references and dance moves to match, but at the heart of the story is a young Indian girl's struggle to be loved and accepted in a white western world. The play tackles themes of cultural appropriation, colonialism and unrequited love.

Indian dancer Meena spends three days a week with Kalayani Aunty, an unrelated dance teacher, preparing for the dance competition at the Lord Ganseh Festival in India. But as her high school Grad 2013 approaches, Meena's desire to be a 'normal' schoolgirl – getting drunk, meeting boys and attending summer festivals – intensifies.

During her dance lessons, she discovers a sense of freedom and escapes into her fantasy world: transforming into her favourite celebrity actress '1994 Miss-World-turned-Bollywood-Superstar, Aishwarya Rai' and embracing the advances of her high school crush, Buddy Cain, a white, popular athlete in her high school.

But Meena's fantasy is a far cry away from reality. Her world comes crashing down when she spots Buddy kissing Candice Paskis, a white blonde-haired student, at the Punjabi market. Meena's heartbreak tears her from the world she knows; she quits dancing with Aunty and begins to perceive her cultural identity as a burden, complaining 'we lose at everything'.

Aunty replaces Meena with her friend Lalita. Meena finds it hard to conceal her jealousy and attempts to sabotage Aunty's plans by using scaremongering tactics on Lalita.

With distance growing between Aunty and Meena, a crush who is in love with someone else and the revelation that Candice is planning to attend the Coventry School of Bhangra with aspirations to become an Indian dancer, Meena is forced to re-evaluate who she is and value her cultural heritage.

Summary (extract)

When their Indian dance is selected for the school assembly and **Candice**, an aspiring Indian dancer, challenges **Meena** about Indian dance moves, **Meena** is forced to reinstate her position.

Meena *turns around and runs into the Natraj statue on her way out. They meet eyes for a moment.* **Meena** *decisively turns away and walks through the doors of her high school in Port Moody.*

So I just decided concentrate on school. Like NO dance, JUST school!

But then … our stupid dance got picked for the stupid school assembly! Remember gym class? The 'dance ensemble'? And Candice. Candice Paskis is all like, (*uses an Indian dance hand gesture*) 'Hey guys, I came up with some new moves. It's like "Indian dance"?' Indian? Hello? I think I might happen to know a little something about 'Indian dance'. And then Candice? Candice Paskis, is all like, 'Hey guys, I saw John Travolta do this one in Pulp Fiction. It's like Aquarius, like the fish-eyes move!' I'll show you fish eyes! It's actually called 'Kartarimukha'.

Meena *demonstrates the bharatanatyam single-hand gesture series in sequence as she speaks.*

It's the fourth mudra in a series of single hand gestures used to storytell in pure classical dance. I mean, let's have a little give and take here! First she steals my Buddy, my Grad 2013 date, and then she wants to steal my dance too? She's just a big STEALER!

Meena *throws her backpack off in a temper tantrum and then stares at it. Beat. Embarrassed,* MEENA *then opens the backpack and takes out her scrapbook, and opens it to a page of choreography notes across from the Aishwarya Rai movie poster.*

But then I went home. And I started to think about how to make the dance good – well, as good as it can be. And I came back really excited, you know? Because there's this problem spot in the dance that no one else could figure out, but I … I actually suggested doing a spin where we all do this!

Meena *performs a series of precise spins.*

But Candice Paskis was all like, 'Um, I don't think they do THAT in Indian dance'. But then Candice's friends who are usually like her yes-men, right? They said that they never thought I could dance like that. So then I showed them some more stuff.

She demonstrates a full Indian dance phrase for the other girls.

Like easy stuff; stuff I've been doing since I was really little. And they just ate it up! And the best part – the best part was? CANDICE PASKIS? Couldn't say anything because she was the odd one out!

Destiny's Child's 'Survivor' begins to play. **Meena** *is in the centre of the gym in the middle of their school assembly. She expertly performs a dance full of spins, intricate hand gestures, and footwork matched to the contemporary beat with complete confidence before her high-school peers.*
Meena *ends in a triumphant classical Indian pose bringing the high-school audience to their feet, showering* **Meena** *in applause.*

From

BOYS WITH CARS

by Anita Majumdar

Boys With Cars, which premiered as a double bill with *Fish Eyes*, was produced by Nightswimming Productions and opened at the Great Canadian Theatre on 14 October 2014. This production was written, choreographed and performed by Anita Majumdar and directed by Brian Quirt. *Boys With Cars* is the follow-up to Fish Eyes and the second part of a trilogy, which also includes *Let Me Borrow That Top*.

Boys With Cars is a one-woman coming-of-age story about a young teenage girl Naznin (referred to in the play simply as Naz). Similar to Meena, the protagonist of *Fish Eyes*, she is also a classically trained Bollywood dancer and attends the same high school; however, her journey unravels in a much darker narrative. Anita Majumdar provocatively juxtaposes the one of the most shocking and highly publicised celebrity headlines of the twenty-first century, the domestic violence between young lovers Chris Brown and Rihanna, with the sexual assault inflicted on the play's lead character, Naz. Majumdar questions our ability to overlook a wrongful act perpetrated by a person based on their beauty, status, talent and sex. The play also tackles themes such as self-acceptance, bullying and hatred.

Set in the small town of Port Moody, teenager Naz dreams of escaping the gates of Port Moody Secondary School to attend the University of British Columbia (UBC). The plays opens in the present with Naz at a wedding waiting for her mother-figure-cum-stage-mum Gustakhi, a stranger who she met at the mall, to arrive. To appease Gustakhi and pay for her keep, Naz performs corny dance routines in the school hall to *Slumdog Millionaire*'s 'Jai Ho' song for white people's weddings, which she rehearses on the cold concrete parking lot due to having no access to a dance studio. She hates peoples watching her perform on stage, especially 'him': ex-boyfriend and wannabe Bhangra singer sensation, Lucky Punjabi, an Irish-Indian who puts on a fake working-class British accent.

The play flashes back to show how Naz became stuck in Port Moody as an Indian wedding dancer. At school, Naz was a wallflower, longing for romance and acceptance from the cool kids at school. Her luck soon changed when she becomes Lucky's girlfriend. She instantly becomes a part of the in-crowd, avoided by other students as a sign of respect. With driver Lucky she experiences a world outside of Port Moody, on their regular road trips.

But when Lucky travels out of town to audition for *Bhangra Idol*, his best friend Buddy makes a move on Naz at the school assembly performance. Before Naz has an opportunity to tell anyone what happened, Buddy tells Lucky that Naz made a move on him. A distraught Lucky breaks up with Naz and leaves Port Moody.

Naz is devastated but has no one to turn to. The popular kids in the school side with Buddy and join him to make her life a living hell at school for what she did to their friend Lucky. After being called to the Principal's office eight times in one month, Naz is asked to study from home to avoid any further disruption. Her parents kick her out of the house, forcing to find work as well as a new home. She rents a basement apartment from Gustakhi and together they run a business where Naz performs dances at weddings. This new arrangement forces Naz to give up her dreams of studying at UBC and leaving Port Moody, but when Gustakhi informs her of Buddy's wedding to Candice she plots ways to seek her revenge. As Buddy's wedding date approaches, Gustakhi tries to discourage Naz by disclosing a secret about her past that leaves Naz dumbfounded.

Summary (extract)

Teenager **Naz** is wearing a hoodie, peacock blue Indian dance skirt and sweat leggings. As she waits for **Candice** and **Meena** to perform for the school's assembly, **Lucky**'s best friend and **Candice**'s boyfriend, **Buddy**, sits beside her. As Destiny's Child's song 'Survivor' plays in the background, **Buddy** covers both his and **Naz**'s legs with his jacket.

Naz *Destiny's Child's 'Survivor' plays, starting meena and candice's dance performance.*

Buddy moves his jacket over both our knees when we start watching Candice and friends dancing to this, like, out-of-nowhere Indian dance by the girls' gym class …

Flash to **Meena** *performing her 'Survivor' dance.*

I'm focusing on Meena, the one Indian girl who actually looks like she knows what she's doing, when Buddy grabs my hand under the jacket …

Naz's *right hand grabs her left wrist,* **Naz** *remains frozen in this wrist-lock dance gesture.*

… and moves it … on him … on his … private … on his body? Do you … understand what's happening? Because I don't. I don't … understand. I keep watching the school-assembly dance while trying to pull my hand back, but Buddy squeezes it there and rolls it in waves, which makes the jacket move. And it's damp – Every time I go over it in my head, I always ask myself, 'Why didn't you use your free hand to pull the other hand away?!' That would be a practical application of Indian dance training! One quick – I keep watching the school-assembly dance. I laser-focus on Candice because there's something in my hand that belongs to her. But watching Candice Indian dance, I feel angry because there's something in her hand that belongs to me. Why couldn't that be me down there? I wish my name was Candice right now and I was down there and she was up here – Why didn't I fight harder? Why didn't my face … my face looked like nothing! Like I was just watching this school-assembly dance like it was nothing! Like nothing was happening!

The 'Survivor' dance ends and thunderous applause rises from the gym bleachers.

The dance ends and Buddy throws away my hand –

Naz's *right hand throws away her left hand, releasing the wrist-lock, and her hands transition into clapping along with the rest of the audience in the bleachers.*

– and stands up clapping. And I'm just sitting there. I just sit there while Buddy whispers in Candice's ear. He spins her around by her waist and kisses her and calls her his bitch –

Naz *clasps her hands and stops clapping.*

I'm so stupid! Stupid for just sitting there, stupid for wearing this skirt, stupid for thinking I was one of 'them' because my boyfriend was! Stupid for sitting with Buddy, stupid for not using my hand, for not … STUPID for just – Where was Lucky? Why did he have to leave that day? Why would he leave me there alone with Buddy?! Why would he – When I needed him the most … WHERE WAS LUCKY?!

From

BLOOD

by Emteaz Hussain

Blood, a co-production between the Belgrade Theatre and British-Asian theatre company Tamasha, premiered at the Belgrade Theatre in Coventry, followed by a regional tour. The play was directed by Esther Richardson with the following cast: Krupa Pattani (Caneze) and Adam Samuel-Bal (Sully).

Emteaz Hussain's first play *Blood* is a witty, poetic and gripping two-hander. This remixed *Romeo and Juliet* tells the love story of two star-crossed South-Asian teenage lovers who, amid violent acts of disapproval from their family members, find a way to stay together. Set in the heart of the Midlands' Pakistani community, Hussain's writing perfectly depicts the language spoken by young people from multicultural inner-city British societies, combining urban slang, Mirpuri-Punjabi and Jamaican patois for the characters of Sully and Caneze. The play captures the complexities of the lives of young people who are forced to negotiate their chosen lifestyles and relationships through social, cultural and religious constraints. In Hussain's play, love becomes the catalyst for change as the couple go to extreme lengths to escape Pakistani gang violence in order to gain freedom and independence.

After meeting in the school canteen, Sully and Caneze agree to go on a first date to Sully's favourite restaurant, Nandos. But like most first dates, things don't always go to plan. Caneze accidently overspills the triple-strength piri piri sauce on her food, admits to being a vegetarian and reveals that her brother is Saif, a notorious Pakistani gang member. Sully is left contemplating if he should pursue a relationship with Caneze for fear of a violent backlash from her brother and his friends. But they both fail to act against their strong feelings for each other, and their forbidden romance begins.

Things go terribly wrong when Saif finds out about their relationship and Sully's plans to take Caneze to Egypt for a short romantic getaway. As Caneze waits for Sully at the airport as planned, Sully is brutally attacked by her brother and his friends and is left wounded in a hospital bed with fractured ribs and death threats.

Sully's family fear for his safety and his brother sends him on a plane to Pakistan. While the two teen lovers are separated, Caneze's amma (mother) grows more ill and is rushed into hospital. Months go by without a word from Sully and after several months, with pressure from family, Caneze reluctantly agrees to marry her brother's friend Yousuf, seeing it as her ticket to freedom. But when Sully returns, appearing outside her bedroom window, she finds it hard to deny her true feelings.

An unexpected visit from her fiancé leaves Caneze violated and fearful of a married life with Yousuf. But to follow her heart, Caneze will need to sever all family ties. When her family become the people she fears the most, Caneze is left to question the price of happiness and if blood is really thicker than water.

Summary (extract)

Sully has revealed the truth about the events that led to his sudden trip to Pakistan and has come back to fight for their relationship. **Caneze** still has love for **Sully** but is set to marry Yousuf. But an unannounced visit from **Yousuf** reveals his true colours and leaves her contemplating her safety and protection.

Caneze   doorbell ringing
an' I weren't expecting no one
when I saw him at the front door, Yousuf, I should've
known better than to let him in, he shouldn't have
been here and I knew it weren't right but sometimes
it's hard to say no to some peoples

She retells the story of **Yousuf**.

he said:

'I come to see you
I'm sorry I shouldn't come round like this
I know it's wrong, I know
but I just got to see you

look, I wanted to ask you something
it's your birthday next week right

oh
sorry I missed it
I wanted to propose properly, sort of on your birthday
though ...'

will you marry me?
I know, but I never done this – have I?
look, I got this magazine
Asian Bride, you read it

could ask for something better
a better venue for the wedding,
we could hire the castle in town

we could have a big party there after the wedding
and write our story in the magazine
look at this ...

Fozia and Alif made in heaven

"we soon started to look for a suitable venue for the wedding and
decided on the Empire Banqueting Suite"

look at the pictures

why not?
we can afford it
it'll be brilliant
we can hire two bands and a DJ
we could arrive in a helicopter

what's wrong with showing off
cos it's always been about showing your money,
if you can't do it on your wedding day when can you do it
doesn't matter where you come from

you got your dress right?
look this guy here made sure his suit matched his bride's
dress
at our party, at the castle
that's when we could …
listen to this
"Ravi had co-ordinated the colour scheme of my outfit
with the venue's décor. Ravi wore a matching designer
sherwani
and later changed into his Armani suit …"

we're getting married
it's all ok,
we're going to spend the rest of our lives together

you'll be all mine soon
everything about you will belong to me

I don't know why you're scared
I'm going to be your husband
it really makes no difference

you should be aching for me

why you playing righteous
little miss shy virgin
don't think I don't know
what you got up to before it got sorted

I know

I don't listen to them rumours
cos you're mine; have always been there
for me, and no one else would touch you, come near you,
not after you been sullied by one of them low-downs
if anyone of them come anywhere near you again
he'd be killed

I'm going to be your husband
and what do you think your mother's going to do
she's my best 'auntie' isn't she?
she wouldn't mind me here
treats me like I'm one of her own
special
Saif knows I'm here
I could give you something if you want
a little something to make you feel better
look, don't look worried
I don't mean to frighten you

Beat.

no need to say anything about my 'visit'

Slight pause.

I should've fought, but I didn't, he ripped my dress and
kept on

Beat.

couldn't tell a soul

Beat.

I tried

Beat.

but

Twenties

From

SHADES

by Alia Bano

Shades premiered at the Royal Court Jerwood Theatre Upstairs in London on 28 January 2009. This production was directed by Nina Raine with the following cast: Stephanie Street (Sabrina), Navin Chowdhry (Zain), Elyes Gabel (Ali), Matthew Needham (Mark), Amit Shah (Reza) and Chetna Pandya (Nazia).

Alia Bano's romantic comedy is about a young liberal-minded Pathan girl's search for the perfect Muslim partner. The play explores the complexities within the secular Muslim communities where the Qur'an and tradition are subjected to interpretation by those living in a multicultural modern British society. Through her unconventional characters, Bano breaks down the stereotyped perception of a Muslim man and Muslim woman, and instead shows the many different individual experiences and life choices, which makes finding the perfect partner almost impossible.

Set in London, female protagonist Sabrina is a university-graduated event planner who is actively searching for a non-traditional, intelligent Muslim man who is not an IT consultant or accountant.

Described as having a 'Bridget Jones status' by her closest friend and flatmate Zain, Sabrina (known as Sab) has been unlucky in love. As she approaches the age of thirty, with her biological clock ticking, she is desperate to find her perfect Muslim husband and convinces gay Muslim best friend Zain to join her at a Muslim speed dating night. The night ends with a disappointing dinner proposition from a cocky, misogynistic yet handsome guy Ali.

When Sabrina is asked to organize a charity event to raise awareness of the injustice occurring on the West Bank, she is paired with a young devout Muslim man named Reza. The two are worlds apart; Reza takes pride in his Islamic faith, praying five times a day, whereas Sabrina enjoys a life of drinking, partying and wearing tight-fitted clothes and miniskirts. Sabrina quickly realizes that there is more to Reza than his Islamic faith and begins to fall for his caring and honest nature. Likewise, the more Reza talks to Sabrina, the more he admires her intellectual mind, spirited nature and witty humour. They both realize that they share a desire to meet someone who does not judge them based on their faith or attire, and feel they have met their match.

But as their feelings grow stronger towards each other, their friends and family members' preconceptions about their choice of partner threaten to create a wedge between them. Ali, who turns out to be Reza's best mate, bruised by having been rejected by Sabrina, is determined to break them up by spreading lies about Sabrina to Reza's sister Nazia. Sabrina's gay pal Zain is also not in favour of the relationship, fearing that Reza will prohibit Sabrina from continuing to have a friendship with him because of his sexuality. But can Sabrina and Reza overcome prejudiced attitudes, lies and cultural expectations to have a chance at true love?

Summary (extract)

Sab (Sabrina) is a young university-educated Pathan, who works as an event planner. She is alone with Muslim devotee Reza as they prepare a fashion show for the upcoming charity event. When **Sab** wrongfully assumes that **Reza** does not listen to music because of his faith, their conversation turns to their perceptions of each other, relationship with Muslims and the Islamic faith.

(The age of the character Sabrina is not indicated in the script; however, based on the information in the text, a suggested age of mid- to late twenties is recommended for this role.)

Sab It's weird, for me it was the other way round. My brother always used to go on and on about how I should dress more like an Asian girl. Wear a scarf on my head so people would know I was a decent girl. And I was like, I know girls who smoke, drink, sleep around, but no one thinks they have because they wear the *hijab*.

Reza *is about to speak, but* **Sab** *continues before he can say anything.*

I know not all the girls are like that. It's really weird, but if my brother had told me to wear boob tubes and a miniskirt, I probably would have worn a headscarf and everything. I nearly wore it just to give my mum some peace from constantly stopping the battles between us.

[…]

I think people should be judged for what they do, and then before I could, I got offered a place at uni and I left home. I'm not really a practising Muslim like you are.

[…]

Like even at uni I felt more comfortable among the non-Muslims because they didn't think a skirt, or the sip of a drink, made me a bad person.

[…]

I know it's wrong but –

[…]

You want to know [What it was like]

[…]

First year of uni.

[…]

A lime Bacardi Breezer. And I had about six of them. […] Smashed. I just wanted to try it. The thing I absolutely hate about Islam is that everything is subject to interpretation. 'Consumption

of alcohol is not permitted.' I'd like to know what the definition
of 'alcohol' is. Like a few years ago we were told, don't wear
perfume or deodorant with alcohol in it. That's just ridiculous.
Now I'm hearing from my aunt, who is actually – I wouldn't say,
'by the book', more 'by the headline' – […] say, 'You can't have
drink in your medicines.' I said, 'Shame – whenever I needed that
little something I'd just down the Benylin.'

Reza *laughs*

Guess I'm not really religious like you are.

[…]

I think you have to have a bit more of a pious nature.

Look all I'm saying is –

[…]

I don't know what I'm saying. I don't know the answer, and
I don't care so long as I don't have to debate it. That's why I
avoided the Islamic Society at university, because they will argue
to death. Anyway. Being tipsy was nice, an escape to a wonderful
place, but, trust me, you're not missing much.

From

AT HER FEET

by Nadia Davids

At Her Feet received a world premiere at the Arena Theatre, at the Hiddingh campus of the University of Cape Town, in September 2002. The play was subsequently performed in 2003 at the Warehouse Theatre for the Cape Town Festival, followed by a South African tour. The play then received an international tour. Most recently it was performed at Southbank Centre, London, 2012, directed by the writer and performed by Quanita Adams.

This powerful one-woman play seamlessly interlaces monologues, poetry and hip hop to present a brutally honest, painful, emotional story inspired by honour killings and the events of September 11th 2001. *At Her Feet* is Nadia Davids' first play, which boldly questions our reactions to the brutality and infringement of human rights issues which takes place around the world and how this impacts on the way we view religions, communities and ourselves.

At Her Feet centres on the stoning of a young Jordanian woman, and the lives of four Capetonian women. The characters are all Muslim and are related, but they are very different from each other: Sara is a university student, Auntie Kariema a housewife, Tahira a travel agent, and Ayesha a radical slam poetess. Each has her own job, responsibilities and views on how a modern Muslim woman should act, dress and interpret Islamic faith, practices and traditions. But when faced with the recent events of the televised documentary of the stoning of women, they are each forced to take a deeper look into their own lives. As the play develops, their narratives become more personal and we get to see the cracks, ugliness and pain hidden behind the veil.

Summary (extract)

This speech is performed by **Azra al Jamal**, a young Jordanian Muslim woman in her twenties, as she is being stoned to death by family members.

Azra Al Jamal   My name is Azra. It means un-pierced peal. It means that I am untouched. My name is for something pure and unsoiled. My name is Azra al Jamal, and I have just been killed. I have sat in the middle of a circle of forty men, and I have just been killed. I have felt my body break in different places, and pieces of bone scrape through skin, because there have been eighty hands throwing countless rocks at me for some time now. I have felt my mouth bleed softly against sand, dry enough to make me choke, too thin for me to clutch.

My name is Azra al Jamal and I have just been killed.

Because I spoke to a man who was not my father/brother/uncle/ cousin, and now my father/brother/uncle/cousin has taken rocks and flung them, knocked me unconscious, smashed my teeth, made me scream and beg and say "I didn't mean to", but I did mean to, and my intention doesn't matter now, because I have no honour. And I have no voice. And it is as though my name, my name, Azra al Jamal means nothing because I have been ground into the sand. Now, curled up in an awkward zero, I am circling my own end. It's hot, and although it is midday, all I can see is night. Bent over, halfway between prayer and nausea, I have been tracing the patterns of the desert sky for hours now. I have watched the stars, seen their geometry, heard them moan anxiously down at me, and felt my insides implode with every hardening blow. I have forgotten my name, so I ask you to remember it.

And somewhere – between voices shouting angrily and hands saving me from a worse fate in the afterlife – I know that it is still light. I remember that it is a clear day – that the sun is hanging persistently at the back of my neck, that light is pouring in over secrets. That there are no shadows, or doorways to hide in, that sharing words, using breath to make sounds, letting a voice come through the folds of this cloth, is not allowed. It is a clear day, lost somewhere in a dark time. It is a clear day. Anyone who walks by now can see what is happening to me.

Do you remember my name?

From

JOSEPHINE AND I

by Cush Jumbo

Josephine and I received its world premiere at the Bush Theatre, London in July 2013. The play was later performed at the Public Theatre at Joe's Pub, New York, opening in February 2015. Both performances were performed by Cush Jumbo.

Winner of the *Evening Standard* Emerging Talent Award, Cush Jumbo's debut one-woman play *Josephine and I* is an outstanding homage to the legendary actress and political activist, Josephine Baker.

Inspired by the glamour, glitz and jewels of the international twentieth-century black superstar, actor-cum-playwright Cush Jumbo delves deeper into the life of Josephine Baker to produce a reimagined interpretation of the key events in Josephine's life for the stage. As the title implies, Josephine's life runs in parallel tracks with the story of 'I', a young starry-eyed modern-day actress called Girl, who lives in London. Girl has idolized Josephine Baker since she was a child, when she first encountered a black leading female in classical old movies – 'And, she wasn't the maid. She was the star.' Josephine's journey begins from her early childhood years in St Louis, Missouri, dancing to the beat of her father's drum, then travelling to New York to perform professionally in Harlem and Broadway, followed by the biggest break of her career – starring in *La Revue Nègre* in Paris.

From humble beginnings to stardom, whatever Josephine puts her mind to, she achieves. This formidable and sadly almost-forgotten leading lady travels the world performing all-singing-all-dancing routines on reputable stages, becomes a spy for the French resistance and later a spokeswoman for the civil rights movement, and adopts a dozen children to live in her stately French chateau. The Girl is inspired by her tenacity, success, glamour and ability to reinvent herself and aspires to reach the same level of success in her lifetime.

But as the play unravels, we are exposed to the ugly side of showbusiness as Josephine and the Girl equally encounter the prehistoric dominant racial prejudice attitudes and gender bias that still remain a constant barrier for black female contemporary actors on their ascendance to fame.

The play seamlessly travels back and forth between the narrative of Josephine and the Girl, introducing multiple other characters they both encounter along the way. In the original production, author and actress Cush Jumbo performs energetic perfected dance routines as Josephine Baker.

Summary (extract)

African American waitress and superstar in the making, **Josephine** has the ambition, drive and passion to succeed and no man is going to hold her back. Married to her first husband **Willie** when she was only thirteen years old, with hopes of having a baby and travelling with **Willie** and the Railroad Company to perform across America, a sudden miscarriage puts a halt to all her plans. She divorces **Willie**.

A year later she gets a new job with the Jones Family Band. But when **Red**, the stage manager of Booker T, hears that scheduled act the Utah Dancing Midgets have missed their train, he desperately needs a replacement dancer for the chorus act. All eyes are on Josephine Baker, a young girl who has been spotted practising the Booker T routine on the streets. Red offers the young waitress her debut dancing gig – an offer she cannot refuse.

Josephine   Red is looking at me.

Red says, 'You.'

I say, 'Yes'.

Red says, 'What's your name?'

I say, 'Josephine'.

Red says, 'You know the chorus girl routine I seen you do?'

I say, 'Uh-huh'.

Red says, 'You reckon you can do that routine now?'

I say, 'Uh-huh'.

Red says, 'You reckon you could do that routine now on the stage of the Booker T?'

I say, 'I gotta think about it'.

Red says, 'Well, if you're gonna be like that … '

I say, 'Outta my way! Which way to the stage?!'

I'm standing in the wings of the Booker T watching the same chorus girls up close! But up close, they look different. They look … old.

And they dance like they just aren't there …

Why would they do that?

They're living my dream!

A costume gets thrown at **Josephine.**

Somebody throws a costume at me –

She puts on the costume as she speaks.

I'm all fired up,

I'm chomping at the bit,

I'm straining at the start,

I'm, I'm, I'm – I'm wearing the ugliest costume I've ever seen in my life. It's eight sizes too big!

But I don't care!

I know the routines inside out and I'm ready.

I'm ready! I'm ready! I'm coming! I'm ready!

Song: *'Cake Walkin' Babies'.*

And now I'm on with the chorus girls and I'm dancing.

I can't believe this, I'm dancing up here!

And check me out, I'm on the Booker T stage.

And check me out, check me out, check me –

What the hell?

Jeering, heckling sounds.

The crowd is jeering, wolf-whistling, cat-calling and heckling.

No wonder the girls look miserable.

No respect, no appreciation, this wasn't glamorous at all.

Is this what I have to look forward to?

No. I want more. I want bigger. I'm getting out. I'm dancing out.

And now I'm leaving St Louis, I'm outta here!

I'm touring with the Booker T Show.

I'm travelling all the time

'Cause I'm a show person now and we are always on the move.

I'm going city to city, we're on the circuit.

There isn't a coloured theatre we don't hit.

We hit Philadelphia.

And I meet Willie.

No! Not that Willie, another Willie, Willie Two.

I don't know why all the men I meet are called Willie.

And what do you know, I'm married again!

What?

He played the trumpet, he knew how to blow.

But Willie Two, he wants me at home.

He wants me to stop dancing.

But I don't wanna stop dancing.

He asks me to stop dancing again.

I say, 'Why?'

He says, 'It's time'.

He says, 'Where is it all leading anyway?'

I say, 'I don't really know'.

He says, 'He wants a family'.

I've always wanted a family.

Maybe I should stop, yeah, maybe this is the end.

She stops dancing.

What's that? What's that?!

Shuffle Along they're calling it.

A brand new, one of a kind, never been done before,

All Black Broadway show.

A what now?

An all black Broadway show.

Willie! This has *never* happened!

This is unbelievable!

This is once in a lifetime

This is it!

I don't care what Willie says.

I'm going to make the cut.

Nobody is going to stop me.

She speaks in a whisper.

Willie breathes real gently at night. More gently than you'd think a guy of his size would. Willie will understand. Willie will know that I love him. I just love the stage more. Goodbye, Willie Howard Baker.

And thanks for my name. Josephine Baker. What a ring …

Hello, *New York*!

From

THE MOUNTAINTOP

by Katori Hall

The Mountaintop was developed during the Lark Play
Development Center Barebones workshop in New York in April
2009 and received its world premiere at Theatre503, London
in June 2009, followed by a transfer a month later to Trafalgar
Studios, London. The London production was directed by James
Dacre, with the following cast: Lorraine Burroughs (Camae) and
David Harewood (Dr Martin Luther King, Jr.). *The Mountaintop*
won an Olivier Award for Best New Play in 2010, and opened in
Broadway's Bernard B. Jacobs Theatre, New York City in October
2011, directed by Kenny Leon, starring Angela Bassett (Camae)
and Samuel L. Jackson (Dr Martin Luther King, Jr).

Katori Hall's play *The Mountaintop* is gripping, imaginative and
hilarious. The play excellently captures the man behind the 'Dr
Martin Luther King' title to reveal him as a human being with
fears, disappointments, insecurities and ego. Hall accomplishes her
intention to humanize Dr Martin Luther King in order to enable
us to appreciate how an ordinary man became one of the world's
greatest revolutionary civil rights leaders, in the hope that we will
be inspired to recognize our own capabilities, strength and power.

The Mountaintop is set in the infamous Lorraine Motel in Room
306, the night before Dr Martin Luther King's assassination.
Earlier that day King delivered a famous speech at the Memphis
church to a congregation of a couple of thousand people. As he
waits in the hotel room for close associate Rev. Ralph Abernathy
to return with his Pall Mall cigarettes, he rehearses the words of a
future speech 'Why America is going to hell', relieving himself in
the motel toilet. But when King returns to the bedroom and calls
for room service to request a cup of coffee, Katori's drama turns
into magical realism.

An unknown mysteriously attractive young maid named Camae
arrives with coffee for King only a few moments after he has
put down the receiver. As luck would have it, Camae smokes

the same cigarettes as King, which she pulls out almost from nowhere. Camae's sassy and straight-talking nature, together with a shared love for Pall Malls, swiftly puts King at ease. Captivated by her beauty and amused by her opposing views on political action, which are more in line with his rival, Malcolm X, the two effortlessly exchange banter and pedestrian conversation.

The atmosphere abruptly changes when Camae accidently refers to King by his birth name, Michael. King's paranoia surfaces and he immediately becomes suspicious of Camae's true identity and intentions. He suspects that she is a spy who intends to tear his family apart by recording their conversation and sending it to his wife, to suggest an act of infidelity. Fearful that he is being set up for the second time, he attempts to throw her out of his motel room. Camae is forced to confess that she is an angel sent to inform and prepare him for his impending death, while King is forced to come to terms with his mortality, failures and regrets. This is a play about dreams, hopes and letting go.

Summary (extract)

King has failed to persuade **God** to extend his time on earth and a call to his wife is unanswered. As he becomes more at ease with the prospect of dying, he begins to reflect on his greatest sacrifices and failures. **Camae** (twenties, Lorraine Motel maid) attempts to console him, reassuring him that he will be remembered as a martyr, but it falls on deaf ears. **King** is convinced that he is a sinner and therefore not deserving of the title of a martyr or saint, unlike her. **Camae** opens up about her past to prove that not all angels are perfect.

Camae   You perfect? Then why should I be? Honey, I've robbed.
I've lied. I've cheated. I've failed. I've cursed. But what I'm
ashamed of most is, I've hated. Hated myself. Sacrificed my flesh
so that others might feel whole again. I thought it was my duty.
All that I had to offer this world. What else was a poor black
woman, the mule of the world, here for? Last night, in the back
of a alley I breathed my last breath. A man clasped his hands like
a necklace 'round my throat. I stared into his big blue eyes, as
my breath got ragged and raw, and I saw the hell this old world
had put him through. The time he saw his father hang a man.
The time he saw his mother raped. I felt so sorry for him. I saw
what the world had done to him, and I still couldn't forgive. I
hated him for stealing my breath. When I passed on to the other
side, God – ooooo, She is more gorgeous than me. She the color
of midnight and Her eyes are brighter than the stars. Her hair
… well … just you wait till you see her hair – God stood there
before me. With this look on her face. I just knowed She was just
soooo disappointed in me. I was just a' cryin', weepin' at her feet.
Beggin' her not to throw me down. All that sinnin'. All that grime
on my soul. All that hatred in my heart. But then I looked up and
saw that She was smilin' down at me. She opened her mouth, and
silence came out. But I heard her loud and clear. 'I got a special
task for you and if you complete it, all your sins will be washed
away.'

I opened my file. And I saw my task was you. What could little
old me, give to big old you? I thought you was gone be perfect.
Well, you ain't, but then you are. You have the biggest heart I
done ever knownt. You have the strength to love those who could
never love you back. If I had just a small fraction of the love you
have for this world, then maybe, just maybe I could become half
the angel you are.

From

HURT VILLAGE

by Katori Hall

Hurt Village had its world premiere at the Signature Theatre Company, New York, in February 2012, directed by Patricia McGregor, with the following cast: Marsha Stephanie Blake (Crank), Nicholas Christopher (Cornbread), Corey Hawkins (Buggy), Charlie Hudson III (Ebony), Ron Cephas Jones (Tony C), Joaquina Kalukango (Cookie), Tonya Pinkins (Big Mama), Saycon Sengbloh (Toyia) and Lloyd Watts (Skillet).

Hurt Village, written by Memphis-born Katori Hall, is based on a real-life housing project (under the same name) located in Northern Memphis, which was subsequently demolished in 2002. Hurt Village was constructed in 1953 by the Memphis Housing Authority with a specific aim to increase the number of white residents in the area. In the 1960s, the demographics of this all-white housing development drastically changed over the years to a predominately African American neighbourhood, due to an increase of dilapidated buildings, together with the sanitation strikes and the assassination of Martin Luther King, Jr. Racial tensions were high, which resulted in white residents moving out of the area. With millions of dollars of damage from the riots and the closure of many businesses, Hurt Village became a neglected, violent, drug-ridden area, reported as the third poorest zip-code in the nation.

Katori Hall's play explores the economic, psychological and educational barriers which left the community broken, excluded and powerless. Hall writes a heart-breaking fictional story about survival, shattered dreams and hope.

At the core of *Hurt Village* is thirteen-year-old Cookie, an intelligent, precocious rapper with dreams of becoming a flight attendant. Cookie opens the play with a rap about the realities of life in Hurt Village as she sees it. Like many of the other characters in the play, Cookie dreams of a life away from the insular, bleak, dangerous world of Hurt Village. Sadly, Cookie exudes all the things her mother Crank only wishes she possessed. Former drug addict Crank had Cookie when she was just thirteen years of age. She has been clean of drugs for three years and makes a poor living from fixing the hair of people who live in the community. Crank is attractive but illiterate, resentful of the bright mind of her daughter who she physically penalizes, an act which is regularly stopped by Big Mama.

Crank and Cookie both live with Big Mama, who, besides her main job as a hospital janitor, is on hand to shield her great granddaughter Cookie from the abuse of her mother. Big Mama took the pair in after she developed a soft spot for Crank because of her resemblance to Buggy's mother, who died from a crack overdose. Unbeknown to the family, Crank is pregnant by Cornbread (Toyia's boyfriend), who has been giving Crank money to help with childcare while Cookie's father Buggy is fighting at war.

Suddenly a soldier (Buggy) enters Big Mama's house. He has returned home early from Iraq a little different from how he left. Now suffering from post-traumatic stress disorder, he takes his medication in secret. It is not long before his grandmother, Big Mama informs him that her housing application has been denied, due to the fact that she earns too much money. With less than two weeks before the residents of Hurt Village have been summoned to leave the area, the family are reliant on Buggy to save the day.

Buggy is forced to return to his life of selling drugs to rescue the family from impending homelessness. He joins forces with Cornbread and the two set out to push Tony C from his position on the million dollar Crack Track by selling drugs on his patch. But as the story unfolds, Buggy has a vendetta against Tony C for the gang-rape of his mother which led to a life of drugs, culminating in her death. This becomes his way to get his revenge. But when the operation goes horribly wrong, resulting in Cornbread in a prison cell, Toyia asks Crank to hold Cornbread's stash of cocaine. Crank reluctantly agrees, but when left alone, the temptation gets the better of her; one taste sends her crashing down to rock bottom.

Summary (extract)

Crank (African American woman, late twenties) has been drug-free for three years. But everything changes after a visit from **Toyia**. **Crank** agrees to hold **Cornbread**'s supply of drugs but fails to resist having a taste. One taste leads to finishing the whole supply. Her relapse sends **Crank** spiralling out of control. Things become obvious to her first love, **Buggy**, after she tries to strip **Cookie** naked to beat her with a belt for refusing to lead the pledge of allegiance at school. **Buggy** protects his child but then notices **Crank**'s irrational behaviour and uncontrollable shakes and twitches. Disgusted by her relapse, he tells **Crank** that she should be ashamed of herself.

Crank How come? You 'shamed of yo'self? You sellin' it.
Sellin' it to e'erbody. This shit got me on lock, maine. Ain't no
runnin' from this shit. You walked out damn near ten years ago
and now you wanna be here? For what? For what, *what*? Dangle
a piece of candy in front of our heart? Make it break a lil' more.
When Cookie was growin' up she would walk 'round here askin'
me, who her daddy was, where her daddy was. I almost wanted
to tell her that I didn't know who her daddy was. I was willin'
to label myself a hoe 'cause I couldn't get her daddy to love me
enough to stick around to love her enough.

[…]

Fuck the money, Buggy. 'Why my daddy don't love me, Ma? Why
my daddy don't send me birthday cards, Mama? Why I got his last
name but I ain't neva seen his face?' Yeah, Buggy. Money don't
answer them questions no matter how hard you try. I got to be
makin' shit up. Did you see how proud she was of you? I'm sure
you bein' a soldier satisfied e'er fantasy in her head. 'That's why
my daddy couldn't be there for me. That's why, he was protectin'
me from terrodom' – or terrorists or whatever the fuck you
niggahs wanna call it. Her daddy was a fighter. Didn't know her
daddy was a fuckin' doughboy, not no hero! Her heart's the spittin'
image of yourn, but you don't see it, do you?

[…]

Well, be the daddy yo' daddy couldn't be for you, my daddy
couldn't be for me, e'er niggah daddy couldn't be for them.

[…]

She gone be messed up if she neva know the other half of her.
Sometimes I look at her and I hate myself. Yeah, I just can't
believe I done brought another lil' black girl into this worl'. This
worl' ain't built fo' beautiful brown black girls. The worl' ignore
her, kick her when it's suppose to love her, bite her when it's
suppose to kiss her, tell her she ugly when she really pretty, rape
her and blame it on her, piss on her stomach, cum on her face and
say that the way to make a dollar, shake what ya momma gave
you, not knowin' that what her mama gave her can't be bought.

That her pussy is priceless. A lil' black girl got a hard load to carry. Sometimes I look at her and wish she ain't never been born. Not because I don't love her but because I love her with all my heart. Now is you gone be the worl' or her daddy? 'Cause I tell ya one thing, all her mama is is a lil' black girl who believed what the world done tol' her. Please take her from me.

[**Buggy** *refuses*.]

Yeah, I know. I just thought. I'd ask.

[…]

(*Shrugging her shoulders.*) That's the one thing that'll do a niggah in. Boredom and chaos, Buggy. Boredom and chaos.

From

WE ARE PROUD TO PRESENT A PRESENTATION ABOUT THE HERERO OF NAMIBIA, FORMERLY KNOWN AS SOUTHWEST AFRICA, FROM THE GERMAN SUDWESTAFRIKA, BETWEEN THE YEARS 1884–1915

by Jackie Sibblies Drury

We Are Proud to Present ... received its world premiere in April 2012 at Victory Gardens Theater, Chicago, Illinois, directed by Eric Ting and starring: Tracey N. Bonner (Actor 6/Black Woman), Bernard Balbot (Actor 1/White Man), Kamal Angelo Bolden (Actor 2/Black Man), Jake Cohen (Actor 3/Another White Man), Travis Turner (Actor 4/Another Black Man) and Leah Karpel (Actor 5/Sarah). This was followed by a New York premiere at Soho Rep in November 2014, with the same director, starring: Quincy Tyler Bernstine (Actor 6/Black Woman), Erin Gann (Actor 1/White Man), Grantham Coleman (Actor 2/Black Man), Jimmy Davis (Actor 3/Another White Man), Phillip James Brannon (Actor 3/Another Black Man) and Lauren Blumenfeld (Actor 5/Sarah). Most recently, the play received its European premiere at the Bush Theatre, London in February 2014, directed by Gbolahan Obisesan, with the following cast: Ayesha Antoine (Actor 6/Black Woman), Joseph Arkley (Actor 1/White Man), Kingsley Ben-Adir (Actor 2/Black Man), Joshua Hill (Actor 3/Another White Man), Isaac Ssebandeke (Actor 4/Another Black Man) and Kirsty Oswald (Actor 5/Sarah).

Award-winning writer Jackie Sibblies Drury's critically acclaimed play was featured in *New York Magazine*'s 'Top 10 Theater Picks of 2012' and received an OBIE Award in 2013.

We Are Proud to Present ... is a harrowing play about the almost-forgotten Herero genocide, which resulted in the massacre of an estimated 65,000 members of the Herero tribe at the hands of German troops in Namibia. With very little information available, especially from the perspective of the Herero tribe, an ensemble cast of six actors (three black and three white) attempt to devise a play about the Herero genocide. For our amusement, Drury

brilliantly conveys the rehearsal process by inserting cliché
moments of actors rehearsing in the play. This play-within-a-play
juxtaposes the personal lives and attitudes of modern-day actors
and the historical characters they are trying to depict on stage.
However, as the play develops, so do the racial tensions in the
rehearsal room, which results in a horrifying ending.

Jackie Sibblies Drury explores the complexities of not only
dramatizing a factual story on very few facts, but attempting to
capture the authenticity of a person's real-lived experience, trauma
and race. Drury leaves no grave unturned in her provocation to
challenge audiences to confront and discuss race in a way that's
not politically correct or safe, but is simply truthful.

We Are Proud to Present ... opens with the fourth wall left slightly
ajar. Actor 6, who considers herself the Artistic Director of the
show, is aware of a few audience members as she nervously
welcomes them to the show. The actors introduce themselves,
adopting a casual and friendly manner; we are then seamlessly
transported into the early stages of a rehearsal process. Equipped
with a handful of letters, a historical overview of the key events
leading to the Herero genocide and a few photographs as stimuli,
the actors start to improvise the play. It's not long before they
begin to question the process, narrative and their abilities –
abruptly stopping a scene to request their motivation and adopting
a Stanislavsky method to act out a sad part in the play by thinking
of their dead cat, then taking the directorial note literally and
performing the role as a cat.

The play takes a sudden turn when Actor 2 notices that their
improvisation, inspired by the letters, gives light to the white
German soldiers but fails to depict or acknowledge the Herero
tribe: 'I think we should see some Africans in Africa.' Actor
4 jumps into the role of Herero and improvises a scene in an
over-exaggerated stereotypical fashion, speaking with a broad
African accent, which angers Actor 2, who takes offence at his
representation of an African man. As the actors continue their
quest to find authenticity and truth behind the Herero narrative, the
lines between the characters in the play and personal attitudes to

race become even more blurred. The play gets darker and darker, closing with an irreversible, painful and extremely uncomfortable ending.

Summary (extract)

A heated conversation about the authenticity of blackness has erupted in the rehearsal room. **Actor 6**-cum-Artistic Director of the show attempts to defuse the situation by disclosing the moment when she first discovered the Herero genocide and how a photograph of a Herero woman who resembled her own grandmother enforced the idea of family, belonging and legacy.

Actor 6   What he's saying is that the whole point of this
whole thing is that
these people aren't so different from us.
Right? Right.
Like, for me the whole idea for this whole presentation
started when I sat down
in my house, in my kitchen
and I opened a magazine
and I saw my grandmother's face
in the middle of a page.
So I read the story around her face,
and the story was about people I'd never heard of,
in a place I'd never cared about.
An entire tribe of people nearly destroyed.
People who looked like my family
And I thought about *my family*.
My father.
My grandmother –
a woman who died before I was born.
And I've missed her my whole life, and I always
wondered what she would have sounded like,
and here she was,
speaking to me through the picture of this Herero
woman. *That* was my way in.
It was like I was having a conversation with my
grandmother.

[…]

Do you see what I'm saying, people?
The woman in that article looked just like my grandmother
and that doesn't happen to me –
I don't belong to a tribe
I don't know where my ancestors were from
I don't have a homeland where people look like me
I'm just British, Black British, and
people tell me I look like other women all the time
but I never actually look like these other women they say I
look like

not really
because to some people
all black women look the same,

But the woman in the article.
She looked like my grandmother.
And suddenly I felt like I have a lineage.
I felt like maybe
I could point to a place
a specific country
a specific homeland
and I could say
there.
My family is from there.
And I found that because my grandmother came to me
and told me about a genocide, where eight out of every
ten people in this tribe
my tribe had been murdered.

From

BLACK JESUS

by Anders Lustgarten

Black Jesus premiered at the Finborough Theatre on 1 October 2013. The play was directed by David Mercatali with the following cast: Debbie Korley (Eunice), Paapa Essiedu (Gabriel), Alexander Gatehouse (Rob) and Cyril Nri (Moyo).

Anders Lustgarten's play *Black Jesus* raises many fundamental questions related to justice, innocence, guilt and retribution. Lustgarten examines the lives of those connected to Robert Mugabe's brutal regime, specifically focusing on Zimbabwe's youth militia called the 'Green Bombers'. The Green Bombers were set up to brutally torture and kill people who were affiliated with the opposing Movement for Democratic Change (MDC). The Mugabe government has fallen and the Green Bombers programme has been abandoned, leaving many of its graduates detained in jails and families destroyed. The country has successfully rebuilt itself, overcoming years of no jobs, no food and a worthless currency. With a fertile future ahead, Lustgarten questions if Zimbabwe can truly move on without confronting and healing the brutalities and injustices of its past.

Black Jesus takes place in Zimbabwe in 2015. Eunice Ncube, working for the new Truth and Justice Commission, is investigating the horrific past crimes enforced by Robert Mugabe's government. She nervously starts her assignment in a high-level detention centre, interviewing one of Africa's most notorious perpetrators, Gabriel Chibamu. Gabriel prides himself as a self-proclaimed Black Jesus who decided who would be saved or condemned. Post-Mugabe, Gabriel finds himself detained for five years without any prospect of a trial.

The two are from different sides of the track. Eunice is university-educated, whereas Gabriel comes from Mufakose, a poor community in Zimbabwe, and was brought up by his mother who dreamt of her son attending university. Gabriel's only route to acquiring education was through Mugabe's National Service

training, the 'Green Bombers' programme. Gabriel's intelligence
and strength made him the perfect candidate. Brainwashed by the
leaders of the camp, who rewarded their students with drugs and
parties, Gabriel opens up about his first mission to publicly beat
his uncle, a MDC sell-out. Eunice interrogates Gabriel about the
other alleged atrocities. But as the truths unfold, Eunice's real
identity is discovered, leaving nobody completely unaccountable
for the suffering carried out under the Mugabe regime.

To make matters worse. Eunice is having an affair with her boss,
Rob Palmer, who is married to a South African woman. Although
it is clear that Rob has no intention of leaving his wife, Eunice
struggles to reject his advances. White Zimbabwean Rob struggles
to be respected and trusted in Zimbabwe. He is subjected to daily
abuse and death threats which eventually prove too much for
him, and without informing Eunice he resigns from his position.
Eunice is informed about Rob's resignation from the newly
appointed Moyo, an apologist, who has no intentions of keeping
her employed.

Summary (extract)

Eunice's true identity has been discovered by **Moyo**, who has
disclosed the fact that she is the daughter of Daniel Shamuyariwa,
the inventor of the Green Bombers, to her client Gabriel Chibamu.
Determined to reassure Gabriel of her intention to help him, she
demands to speak with him for one last time.

Eunice   I came to tell you the story of my father. Will you let me tell you his story? My father was a thinker. He was a quiet, gentle man. Stiff in company, like new shoes. Warm and soft like old slippers with his children. I loved him very much.

He was a supporter of the revolution in the way he knew how. He could not live among the rats and steel bars of the imprisoned, nor the goats and wood smoke of the foot soldiers, but what he could do was think. He designed many of Zanu's best social policies. The Old Man took a shine to him.

As a child, the big men I saw on television would come to my house and have tea. I thought this was normal, that every child shared a biscuit with Robert Mugabe, that it was something he did when he got bored of his office. He would ask me to fetch him the sugar, and he would let me take a cube from the bowl as a treat, and I felt special, not because I knew who he was but because an adult was paying me attention. My father watched me like a hawk every step of the way, and I will never forget the expression on his face – pride and happiness, but with a bilious green slick of fear over it. I always thought it was my fault, that I was doing something wrong that spoiled his pleasure. But I could never find out what it was.

Those were the good days of Zimbabwe, our days in the sun. Later on, the atmosphere changed and the house grew colder. No more lines of black government cars in the street, their chauffeurs squatting in the drive to throw dice or dominos. No more shared biscuits with the Old Man. I went away to university, but whenever I returned it was to the sound of shouting matches, my mother's voice raised in anger and my father's in defence. Phone calls where the other man was very, very angry. A build of pressure like before a thunderstorm. And then one day, a gap in the hallway where my father's coat lived. He had gone away for a few days, my mother said. Just a few days. And then a few more, and a few more, and more.

A month later, my father rang me, and told me the whole story. That one day the Old Man had called him into his study and asked him to undertake a new project. The mobilisation of unemployed

youth. To give them something to do, to help them 'fulfil their potential'. A project called the Green Bombers.

[...]

He tried [to refuse]. He told the Old Man he did not think he was suited to the task. And he told him if he did not take it, the job would fall to Endurance Moyo.

[...]

He never intended for you to be used in the way you were.

From

THE WESTBRIDGE

by Rachel De-lahay

The Westbridge was first professionally performed at the Bussey
Building, Peckham Rye as part of the Theatre Local season, in
November 2011. The play later transferred to the Royal Court
Theatre in London. Both productions were directed by Clint
Dyer and performed by Ryan Calais Cameron (Andre), Chetna
Pandya (Soriya), Jo Martin (Audrey), Ray Panthaki (Ibi), Paul
Bhattacharjee (Saghir), Fraser Ayres (Marcus), Daisy Lewis
(Georgina), Shavani Seth (Sara), Samuel Folay (Boy) and Adlyn
Ross (Old Lady).

The Westbridge by Rachel De-lahay (formerly *SW11*) and *Sucker
Punch* by Roy Williams were joint winners of the Alfred Fagon
Award for Best New Play of the Year in 2010. This was followed
by a rehearsed staged reading of both plays, directed by Simeilia
Hodge-Dallaway at the Cottesloe Auditorium at the Royal
National Theatre.

Rachel De-lahay's debut play *The Westbridge* is a fiercely
provocative exploration of the racial tensions between the
Black and Asian communities in Britain. Set on the Westbridge
council estate in Battersea, South London, both communities
overlook their inherited prejudiced attitudes to live harmoniously,
developing strong friendships and romantic relationships. But in
common with most estates, it does not take long for rumours to
spread from one apartment to the next. So when a young black
boy is accused of raping a fourteen-year-old Asian girl, the
news quickly becomes hot local gossip, triggering deep-rooted
prejudices, dividing the community and resulting in an
uncontrollable explosive street riot.

At the heart of this story is a young interracial couple, Pakistani
Soriya and African Caribbean Marcus, who are both mixed
race. They have recently moved in together and while they
adjust to living under the same roof with Soriya's best friend

and housemate George, the recent events threaten to push their relationship even further to the limit.

As the play develops, we discover that Marcus's childhood friend, sixteen-year-old Andre is the alleged culprit. Marcus is convinced that Andre is innocent but like Andre's mother, who kicks him out of the house after hearing the allegations, Soriya is not so sure.

A conversation with an elderly Indian woman, who suggests that Asian girls should be for Asian men only, claiming that integration creates more confusion, leaves Soriya questioning her own relationship with Marcus.

With the growing pressure and scrutiny from family members and the community, their relationship is at breaking point, the protest has begun, and teenager Andre has nowhere to hide. But when Marcus spots Andre kissing a young Asian girl in a private garage on the Westbridge estate, the truth is unravelled. Suddenly, the spotlight is back on Soriya and Marcus – but is there too much water under the bridge for them to reconcile?

Summary (extract)

The rape allegation is spreading fast in households on the Westbridge estate and on Blackberry messenger. A distressed and exhausted **Soriya**, a twenty-year-old mixed race white-Pakistani girl, has taken refuge at her father's house away from her boyfriend **Marcus**, to escape the community's gaze and relentless criticism about their interracial relationship. The words from an elderly Indian woman whom she helped with her shopping bags has left **Soriya** doubting the success of interracial relationships, including her own. **Marcus** has heard from **George** that **Soriya** is upset and arrives at the house to find **Soriya** standing outside smoking.

Soriya   Why are we? What makes us so special? Everything
we have in common is in line with our age. We like the same
music, the same films, but that's it. We've grown up in completely
different cultures, different worlds and I just worry they don't
mesh together all too good.

[…]

Our parents are respecting our choices. I'm sure if they could
make the decision for us they wouldn't wish this.

[…]

I'm not like you, OK? I'm not cool with who I am! I grew up my
whole life being so grateful I was raised with my dad. People stare
at me when they can't place where I'm from. They know I'm not
white but after that they get stuck. When I'm with my dad they
understand. We're Asian. I have an identity. And I love it. I love
belonging to a large family that bickers over the dinner table. I
love getting dressed up to go to our many relatives' weddings. I
love Dad forcing us to watch crap soaps on ARY when we have
dinner round his despite all the protests to just put *EastEnders* on.

[…]

I'm scared you'll change that.

[…]

No I'm upset 'cause I've just realised I don't think mixing races
works. […] I know it's a horrid thing to say, but it doesn't mean I
can stop thinking it.

I'm gonna have an arranged marriage. […] Not right away but
it's what I want. I want to have Pakistani children for a Pakistani
husband. I don't want my children to be as confused as I am.

[…]

I'm sorry.

From

KHANDAN

by Gurpreet Kaur Bhatti

Khandan premiered at Birmingham Rep Theatre, England in May 2014, before touring to the Royal Court Theatre, London in June 2014. Both productions were directed by Roxanna Silbert with the following cast: Preeya Kalidas (Reema), Sudha Bhuchar (Jeeto), Zita Sattar (Cookie), Lauren Crace (Liz), Rez Kempton (Pal) and Neil D'Souza (Major).

Khandan is a heart-wrenching tragedy about love, ambition and cultural traditions, set in the suburb of a city in England in the Sikh household of the Gill family. Members of the family struggle to balance their personal desire for freedom with family and religious expectations, as they navigate a life in England.

Widowed matriarch Jeeto grieves over the recent loss of her husband, who died as a result of alcoholism and excessive working. Jeeto has spent several years making sacrifices for her family and now dreams of retiring to the family home in Punjab. But before she leaves, Jeeto is determined for eldest son Pal to follow in his father's footsteps by taking on the responsibility of the family business, land in Punjab and his uncle Chacha.

The only problem is that Pal sees the family shop and house in Punjab as a burden. His feelings for the family business have been blighted by the eighty-hour work shifts which sabotaged his education, freedom and quality time with his parents. Pal has no intention of visiting the family home and therefore has little regard for the house or relatives in Punjab.

Pal's deep-rooted resentment influences his decision to close the shop for the first time on Christmas Day, against the wishes of his deceased father, which angers his mother and girlfriend, Liz. Liz and Pal's attempts at trying for a baby have been unsuccessful, which is not lost on Jeeto, who, besides having two teenage granddaughters (from her daughter Cookie and husband Major), desperately desires a grandson. Liz wants to try IVF but Pal has reservations.

A letter arrives from Chacha (Pal's uncle) who resides in Punjab, requesting the family's help to support their cousin Reema's move to England in search for a better life. Reema's husband Jiti's drug addiction has worsened, which has put all their lives in jeopardy. After receiving pleas from his mother to help Chacha, Pal reluctantly agrees.

Pal secretly sells the shop to gain some of the capital needed for his half-baked business plan to open a nursing home. Liz is left questioning the future of their relationship when he refuses to use any of the money from the shop on IVF.

Reema arrives from Punjab, an attractive, strong-minded, savvy school teacher who 'speaks better English than Pal', with dreams of owning her own bookshop. Reema astutely sees Pal as her ticket to obtaining freedom, a Masters in Business Administration and her own business. She agrees to help with his business plans on the condition that he gives her a loan for her MBA degree. Pal is desperate to prove himself to his family and he accepts Reema's help. But things suddenly go downhill when the financial investor, Uncle Manjit walks away from the project, leaving the renovations incomplete, bounced salary cheques and a broken man. Pal's drinking becomes excessive and his actions become erratic. One of his many drinking episodes results in a heated moment of passion and a baby. With desperation for more money, he has to choose between selling land that has existed in his family for generations and keeping his newborn son.

Summary (extract)

Reema, a qualified school teacher in her late twenties, has recently arrived from India and is already feeling the pull between her homeland and her dreams. As she consumes whisky from a glass, she divulges a disturbing memory which caused her to leave her drug-addicted husband **Jiti**, beloved father-in-law **Chacha** and birthland India. She speaks to her cousin and love-interest **Pal**.

Reema   (*Beat.*)

Can I tell you something? … Something I haven't told anyone.

Pal *nods.* **Reema** *watches* **Pal** *uneasily, walks round the room with her drink. Stops.*

Once, before Jiti left, he had been playing cards with some men from the village. He lost the game and owed them money.

Late one night I was sleeping and these men came to the kauthee [house]. They wanted their money but Jiti had gone out drinking, he was taking nushih [drugs] by then. I heard Chacha's voice and shouting on the verandah. I got out of bed and went outside. The men were drunk and one of them grabbed me, the others laughed and this man started pulling at my clothes, Chacha shouted at them to stop but they wouldn't.

I was screaming. Chacha went inside. They carried on laughing and … my hair came loose. The next thing I knew, there was a noise like a bomb and the man, the one who was holding me, fell back. I looked up and there was Chacha with his rifle. He shouted at them to go, to stay away from his land. The others took the dead one and went. They never came back. Chacha started crying and cursing Jiti. He said, you are my daughter now kureeh [girl]. You are my izzat and I am yours. We will protect each other's honour.

He did the right thing. And I swore I would do the right thing by him. But now … if I leave here, his izzat will be destroyed.

(*Beat.*)

He is owed better than that.

(*Drinks.*) I don't know what to do.

From

CRASH

by Pamela Mala Sinha

Crash premiered at Theatre Passe Muraille in Toronto on 1 May 2012, directed by Alan Dilworth and performed by the author Pamela Mala Sinha (The Girl). The character of The Girl also plays Constable Blier, Krista, Doctor, Little man and Therapist. After being named Best New Play at the 2012 Dora Awards, the play was remounted the following year on 26 September 2013 at Theatre Passe Muraille in a co-production with Necessary Angel Theatre Company, with the same cast.

Pamela Mala Sinha's powerful play describes the aftermath of a sexual assault which causes a young woman to suffer from post-traumatic stress disorder (PTSD), affecting her life and the relationship with her family and God forever. Based on the author's personal experience, this harrowing one-woman play is courageously honest as it graphically details a horrific rape committed against a young woman by a serial rapist. From the language through to the haunting events narrated in the play, Sinha astutely articulates the psychological and physical trauma from the perspective of a person with PTSD. Written in the third person, the unnamed character refers to herself as the 'Girl', distancing herself from reality as she battles with survivor guilt for not fighting back and is tormented by recurrent thoughts, images and memory loss as she struggles to remember the face of her attacker. Sinha uses this poignant piece to raise the awareness of PTSD and to support the many other women who are left feeling powerless, guilt-ridden and unheard. Contrary to our desires for resolution and justice, this play depicts a realistic situation which is more aligned to the experience of the majority of rape survivors who continue a life with no closure, justice or peace.

It's been a year since the death of the Girl's father and as family and friends gather for the memorial, the Girl freezes on the landing of the stairs above them. The loss of her father has evoked another memory of loss which took place over seven years ago, causing a young, free-spirited, pious woman to lose her sense of identity, innocence and strong relationship with God. We enter into the Girl's memory as she takes us on a non-linear journey of her life.

The Girl has a flashback of a childhood memory; she sees a home-made Hindu temple, which she created when she was a child out of a plastic milk crate, a place where God was forever present. She was raised in a liberal family who respected other religions, regularly attended the temple, but were more inclined to follow the teachings of Sri Ramakrishna and his wife Sarada Devi. The girl describes an enjoyable and pleasant childhood with her parents and brother, who are amused by her dedication to praying a thousand times a day.

But things take a drastic turn when the Girl moves away from home for the first time, securing an apartment in Montreal. Filled with anxiety, she seeks comfort in her temple which is deliberately placed in her bedroom, so it's the first thing she sees when she wakes up, just as it was at home. While the Girl is sleeping, she hears the sound of a crowbar forcing the front door of the apartment open. A stranger enters her bedroom, where the Girl is hiding under the covers rather than trying to escape, lying there silently with hopes that the intruder will not notice her. But he goes directly into the bedroom, places a pillow over her head and sexually assaults the Girl. He leaves without her seeing his face. The Girl is traumatized and overcome with inexorable guilt for not being able to identify her attacker for her own and other women's safety, as well as the pain this tragic event has caused to her family, especially to her father whose health is rapidly deteriorating.

Through the support of her family and years of therapy, the Girl is able to recall what happened on the night, with the exception of what her attacker looked like, a constant torment in her life.

This play is not about resolutions, because in these cases there are none; instead the main message in the piece is about the unimaginable strength of family love that can enable a person to stay alive despite experiencing some of the toughest and darkest moments in their life.

Summary (extract)

The **Girl** explains how her relationship with men has changed since the night she was sexually attacked. Without the knowledge of the identity of her attacker and pent up with resentment for not fighting back, she confesses to intentionally enticing men while equipped with a weapon to regain a sense of power and control in her life.

Girl Can't remember isn't the same as forget. That's the problem. Forget is, don't want to remember. Can't remember is, don't want to forget.

Sometimes during a Black, the girl would go to bars to find men. She'd carry a large knife in her knapsack.

(*She approaches the door. When she opens it, music blares and she is enveloped in a red light. She walks through the door, closing it behind her. The music is muted again. She emerges behind the stage left stairs. As if inside the 'club'; she carries a bag slung over her shoulder.*)

Within five minutes some guy would always come up and start talking. She'd talk back, but it was like she wasn't even there … just watching it all happen from the other side of the room. Watching him try to pick her up, try to impress her – the whole time thinking, is he big enough? Strong enough? (*Pause.*) Mean enough?

Because last call would be in about half an hour of getting there, the girl would suggest they go someplace else … Someplace else was always the lakeshore.

(*The song and club sounds plays louder as she dances towards the 'lakeshore' downstage.*)

(*Dancing.*) No one was ever down there at two or three in the morning – at least not the part the girl wanted them to go: the far end, where there's nothing. No ice cream stands, no boardwalks, nothing. You could do anything to a person down there and no one would ever see you.

(*As she spins into a seated position, the music fades – still present but distorted.*)

Sitting, she leans back slightly, leaving one hand free near the open bag beside her.

(*The stage grows darker, with only a spot of light on her.*)

He would have to start. If he didn't start, it wouldn't count. The girl would give the man every reason to believe she was really into it and then – then, when there was no reason to stop – NO. She'd say no, he'd beg, C'mon, baby … she'd say no again, he'd get angry, Are you fucking KIDDING me?! He'd be really angry by now because she'd led him on all this time and because he was so turned on and frustrated and PISSED OFF all at once he'd – force her. He'd – force her to do it even though she said no –

And then – only then – or it wouldn't count / (*Her hand reaches towards her bag.*) Force her or it wouldn't count / (*Body tenses as she waits for it, hand inside her bag.*) …

But none of them ever did. They were all nice men. All they wanted was her number.

(*Pause.*)

She removes her hand from the bag.

It never mattered to the girl that they hadn't caught him. Nothing mattered then.

The girl's parents could only find one hospital where women like her could stay to get help. It was in L.A.

(*We hear the buzz of fluorescents and electricity as a 'light' outline of a bed appears downstage right. She steps down towards it.*)

Stupidstupidstupid girl.

(*A black blanket drops from the ceiling and onto the bed with a crash – triggering the* **Girl***'s memory of* **Krista**.)

Krista   (*Picking up the blanket she lays it on the bed.*) Hi, I'm Krista! I'll help you unpack –

Girl   (*Arms half crossed.*) Wow, thought the girl, they help you unpack here. Krista picks up a gigantic bottle of Chanel No.5,

Girl   My father gave me that for Christmas,

Krista   (*Adopting a gesture.*) Ohhh, that's so sweet. I'll have to take it for now though –

Girl   Why?

Krista   Just – how we like to do things around here …

Girl   Oh, the girl gets it – she might try to kill herself again so take away anything that's glass. There go the scissors, razor – Okay, she gets that – sewing kit, blow dryer?

Krista   Okay, you're all set – I'll see you in a bit!

Girl   This is so stupid … the girl walks over to the window she can't jump out of and waits for something to happen. (*Pause.*) Her period. Shit. (*She finds a black tampon in her pocket.*) Thank god … When Krista sticks her head back in –

Krista   Just wanted to let you know that dinner's – oh. I should've taken that/

Girl   /What? This?

Krista   Just go on over to the nurse's station, George'll give you a pad/

Girl   /The two hundred pound bald man who's picking his nose right now – I have to ask HIM for a pad? Krista moves towards her –

Okay could you just – I mean I don't get it – you think … what – ? I mean, really – what would I do with it, like, stuff it down my throat or – ? Krista takes the tampon and leaves …

The **Girl** *'follows' her out.*

Girl   Well you know what, Krista? Hey – Krista! Know what? If I did want to stuff it down my throat – all you'd have to do is PULL THE GODDAMN STRING!

(*Lights switch off and then, with the buzz of the fluorescents, switch on again revealing the* **Doctor**.)

The Doctor knew without looking the girl would be there: at the far end of the couch, legs curled under a blanket. She had to be there – drama therapy was mandatory. She tried to get out of it at first;

(*As the* **Girl**.) Banging the shit out of something with a big foam bat isn't going to do anything for me – it's called 'substitution' and I do it for a LIVING. He thought that was pretty clever. He agreed to let her come as an observer. That was over a month ago. Now she comes willingly to support her friends … broken women determined to die helping each other live. Only this one didn't want to die – she wanted to kill herself. Because she pulled the covers over her head. Because that's all she did.

(*She sits down on a stair, looking downstage at the* **Girl**.)

Doctor   (*Hands on knees.*) What's the sin?

Girl   (*Hands drop between her knees.*) Huh?

Doctor   The sin. (*Pause.*) If I told you there was a girl – just there – (*Gesturing downstage.*) She's sleeping – when all of a sudden there's a crash – a really big one. She doesn't know what's happening because she's sleeping – but then all of a sudden she realizes it's inside – it's inside her house – she doesn't know what to do there's no time so she/

Girl   /there's time

Doctor   What? Okay … okay, there's time … for what?

Girl   Jump.

Doctor   Jump – ?

Girl   Out the fucking window.

Doctor   The third floor window.

Girl   There's hangers in the closet – why doesn't she scratch his ugly eyes out? Why doesn't she fight him no matter how big or armed or crazy he was because then at least she'd be dead from FIGHTING rather than lying there like an idiot with the covers over her head thinking he wouldn't see you he'd see an empty unmade bed because you were so thin and small and still you STUPIDSTUPIDSTUP –

(*The* **Girl** *is cut off by a blackout and the sudden crash of a heavy steel door slammed shut.*)

But the Doctor knows as he slams the door shut this unforgiving girl, seven years away from that night and safe as she is here in this room –

(*A spot lights up on the* **Girl***; the blanket from the 'bed' now over her head.*)

Will do it again.

(*She pulls the blanket down.*)

Peek-a-boo … a baby's first believing. A terror so big … if I can't see you, you can't see me.

(*The light fades out.*)

(*The outline bed lights emerge in the darkness as the* **Girl** *lies down.*)

As the girl falls asleep that night, something moves inside her.

(*Long pause.*)

She jolts awake. (*The blue reflection of a rearview mirror suddenly appears across her eyes.*

We hear a car in motion. The sound is from the inside of the car.)

Driving from her friend's house on de Bienville to her new apartment on St. Denis. Two big suitcases in the trunk and a box beside her in the back. It's only three blocks away but he's not mad –

It's not too far … The next right – Just here, on the corner – (*The car speeds up.*) Uh – right here is fine … (*The car keeps moving.*). This is great, thanks. (*The car come to a complete stop.*) He offers to carry her suitcases up but to be safe she tells him to leave them on the landing, I can manage from there, because she doesn't want him to see which door is hers.

(*Pause.*)

He saw.

(*Music fades up as the light on her eyes fades out and she moves stage left, entering the 'courtyard'.*)

Instead of leaving her building, he lets himself into the inner courtyard,

(*Three red doors appear above her, stage right.*)

And counts out the corresponding back door on the fire escape. He looks for another way out. (*She looks at the upstage door.*) He sees it: the steel door off the courtyard. The boiler room. Going in, he sees it has another door that leads directly onto an alley.

(*The door slams shut, lights out.*)

(*A spot appears sharply on her. A cyclical loop of sound builds and builds with each new memory.*)

She wants to tell – she wants to scream what she wants to tell because for the first time she has something to tell – she couldn't remember the name of the company but it was only one of three in the book and she remembers the number she called from, the time of the order, the date of the order, the point of pickup and the address of her destination. She remembers all of it and all of it would be on record because she didn't flag the cab she ORDERED IT.

(*With a crash the crowbar appears, ending the looping sound. Each image appears as she names them.*)

Crowbar, cigarettes, lighter, fingerprints, blood type, dirty taste, dirty smell, his laugh …

Still no face … But what she knows now, will change everything.

From

THE FEVER CHART

Three Visions of the Middle East

by Naomi Wallace

The Fever Chart: Three Visions of the Middle East was produced
in 2008 at New York's Public Theater as part of the Public
Lab series. It was directed by Jo Bonney, with the following
cast: *Vision One: A State of Innocence*: Lameece Issaq (Um
Hisham Qishta), Arian Moayed (Yuval) and Waleed F. Zuaiter
(Shlomo). *Vision Two: Between This Breath and You*: Waleed F.
Zuaiter (Mourid Kamal), Natalie Gold (Tanya Langer) and Arian
Moayed (Sami Elbaz). *Vision Three: The Retreating World*: Omar
Metwally (Ali).

Naomi Wallace's trilogy of short, provocative and deeply moving
plays about loss is set in various locations in the Middle East. *The
Fever Chart* comprises three stand-alone stories all based on real
experiences, portraying a snapshot of some of the most difficult
and harrowing events, including being forced to face enemies
and even death itself. Each vision (play) is kept minimalistic with
a bare stage and a few simple hard chairs; the events play out
effortlessly, with no resolution, the same way as life itself. Like
the characters on the stage, the audience are helpless, incapable of
finding solutions to the ever-growing harsh realities of living in a
war-torn country.

The Fever Chart opens with *Vision One: A State of Innocence*,
set in something resembling a zoo but more silent, empty, in
Rafah, Palestine in 2002. The three characters in the play become
the caged animals, trapped in a barren and bleak world unable
to escape their past actions, memories and death. Yuval, the zoo
keeper, is unsure how he arrived at the zoo but is keen to maintain
the order of silence by killing any animal, child or adult that
makes a singing or gurgling sound. Shlomo, the architect, wants
to carry out his work, but is restricted by the soldiers who refuse
to let him pass the checkpoint. But an older, rebellious, fearless
Palestinian woman, Um Hisham, is haunted by a memory that

supersedes their daily grind. Um Hisham is mourning the death of her child Asma, who was killed by an Israeli bullet to the chest as she fed the pigeons on the roof. The grieving mother, distraught that her daughter died alone, has lost her faith in God and spends every day visiting the zoo. As the story about Asma unravels, so does her connection to Yuval; she informs him that he was also shot in her house by Israeli soldiers after he stopped them from beating her husband and then accepted a cup of tea, which resulted in the soldiers killing him, arresting her husband and bulldozing her house. Suddenly the place becomes a vision of purgatory, binding a Palestinian woman and a Tel Aviv Israeli man together by their experience of loss.

Vision Two: Between This Breath and You is set in a clinic waiting room in West Jerusalem, present day. Mourid, a Palestinian father, arrives at the private clinic two hours after closing time, demanding to see nurse Tanya Langer. The newly appointed mopper does his best to obstruct Mourid from seeing the nurse so that he can retire for the day, without any joy. The calm, straight-talking Tanya Langer enters the waiting room after working on her feet for ten hours and reluctantly agrees to give Mourid five minutes of her time. Unable to find anything medically wrong with Mourid, she soon becomes suspicious of his intentions and demands that he leave. But Mourid reveals personal information about Tanya's unqualified nursing status that puzzles her, as she is due to receive her qualifications in eighteen months' time. The events become more unsettling for Tanya when Mourid talks about his deceased son Ahmed and the real reason why he travelled from the West Bank to West Jerusalem to seek her out. Mourid believes that his Palestinian son is living through the young Israeli nurse literally and figuratively, due to a double lung transplant carried out five years ago after Tanya was diagnosed with cystic fibrosis. Tanya is quick to dismiss the allegations, but when Mourid talks profoundly about her disruptive sleeping patterns, recurring nightmares of suffocation and ways of coping with her erratic shortness of breath, she has no choice but to believe him.

Vision Three: The Retreating World is a monologue from an Iraqi bird keeper named Ali from Baghdad. Ali addresses the audience before the International Pigeon Convention.

Summary (extract)

The monologue selected from *The Fever Chart* has been extracted from *Vision Two: Between This Breath and You*. **Tanya**, a twenty-year-old Israeli nurse, has been informed by **Mourid** that she is carrying a part of his deceased son **Ahmed**. To convince her that he is telling the truth, he asks his son to reveal himself, which causes **Tanya** to struggle for breath, until he requests his son to stop. After a few moments **Tanya** begins to breathe normally. Stricken by anger, she takes the opportunity to confront **Mourid**, who has over-romanticized the situation, with a few home truths about how the lung transplant changed her life in a negative way forever.

Tanya   Do you know, Mr Kamal –

Do you know, Mourid, why my fiancé left me? When I told him about the transplant, he said he couldn't bear to make the investment. The average life span of a lung transplantee is six years. I'd done nearly five when I met him.

Half of all patients die within five years after transplant, from infection and chronic rejection. I will probably die because of the toxic effects of the immunosuppressant medicines. It's extremely common.

In these last few months, at times, without warning, I have difficulty breathing. Sometimes, as you witnessed just now, when I am under pressure, for a few moments I lose my capacity altogether. But then it returns. It hardly frightens me anymore.

There is nothing I haven't tried.

Let's say that for a moment, just a moment, that I accept the preposterous notion that my donor was your son –

Then it would be true that I carry with me a piece of. Ahmed. Your son. You like that idea: a piece of Ahmed inside me.

(**Mourid** *nods yes.*)

In fact I'd say you are intoxicated with the idea, that it gives your entire being a shape and focus you would not have otherwise. Otherwise, you'd be just a bag of liquid grief – we could pick you up, poke a hole in the bottom, and you'd just spill away. But imagine the implications here – your son inside me – somehow alive inside me.

(*She sings the rest of the refrain from 'Every Breath You Take,' picking up where* **Mourid** *left off.*)

That would mean he accompanies me. Participates with me. Enjoys with me.

When I laugh, your son laughs. When I sing, your son sings.

(**Mourid** *joyously sings the song. Then they sing it together with vigour.*)

But that would also mean your son was present last night. That's why I am especially tired today. I was awake till four a.m. I picked a stranger up after work. A sweet, eager young man. He fucked me so hard I thought he'd break me in half.

Don't worry. Things went smoothly. Your son gave me good air when I sucked cock. Good Jewish cock.

And let me tell you, I do the deep-throat thing and I need all the oxygen I can get. To cut it short: when I fuck an Israeli, your son fucks an Israeli. And when I have a good orgasm, your son –

(**Mourid** *cries out. He rushes at* **Tanya** *threateningly, as though to hurt her.* **Tanya** *holds her ground. But then* **Mourid** *stops himself, and turns away. He takes a few steps as if to leave.*)

And that's not all I do, Mr Kamal.

(**Mourid** *stops, listening to her with his back.*)

I don't have a steady boyfriend now. Vigorous activity tires me a little more each day. My family, they pretend I'm well. Denial is their elixir. 'Tanya will outlive us all,' my father says. I visit with them less and less. On my break here at work, I usually go to the park. I close my eyes and sit very still until I am no longer there, just the breathing. Just the breathing. And all the world is condensed into the fuel of oxygen, sliding in and out of my chest like the hands of God, working me, working my clay into a form that has no material existence, but is as solid and as palpable as this flesh. What is a good heaven? Yes. I'm afraid. But I imagine it to be a place of floating, where breathing is a continuous, circular motion, unchecked by the dependencies of this world. (*Beat.*) That space where exhalation ends, before the next breath begins. That's where I want to – Where I want to – What is the dream I keep having, of falling and suffocation? How do you know about my dreams?

From

FIREWORKS (Al'ab Nariya)

by Dalia Taha

translated by Clem Naylor

Fireworks premiered at the Royal Court Jerwood Theatre Upstairs in London, in February 2015. This production was directed by Richard Twyman, with the following cast: Eden Nathenson (Lubna), Shakira Riddell-Morales (Lubna), Sirine Saba (Nahla), Shereen Martin (Samar), Yusuf Hofri (Khalil), George Karageorgis (Khalil), Saleh Bakri (Khalid) and Nabil Elouahabi (Ahmad).

Through Taha's play we realize that childhood innocence is hard to sustain when you live in war-torn Palestine. Set in Gaza City during one of the most vicious Israeli invasions in the early twenty-first century, the story focuses on two families who both struggle to shield their young children from the brutal realities that exist just outside their apartment block. With recent bombing of school-shelters and the daily deafening sounds of bombs (referred to as fireworks by their parents) filling the air, the apartment block becomes their only place of safety. As the siege continues to intensify, the parents' attempts to pacify their children's fears and escape the harsh realities of war through imaginative play and fairy-tale-like stories fail miserably. One can never underestimate the high receptiveness of a child, as both Lubna and Khalil prove they are far more knowledgeable about the atrocities of war and the reason for the big bags which sit under the eyes of those who grieve. Dalia Taha's play *Fireworks* shows how war denies the strongest instinct of a parent to protect their children and thus, inevitably the roles between parents and children switch, resulting in a world where the children become parents and parents become children.

Set in a small Palestinian town, *Fireworks* tells the story of the last two remaining families to reside in the same apartment building. The protagonist is a bright twelve-year-old girl, Lubna, who lives with her mollycoddling father and her grieving mother. It's been six months since the death of her brother Ali, shot by a soldier for no reason. The play opens with Lubna casually telling her dad about the song she wrote in her head, about someone getting shot; we realize later that this is a premonition. But when her father quickly corrects her speech to mask the unimaginable horrors encountered on the outside world by replacing the word 'shot' with 'martyred' – along with the more digestible narrative of a martyr who does not feel pain when they die; instead they are greeted by angels, who give them wings so they can fly back to earth and connect with their loved ones in their dreams – we see a parent's desperate and almost impossible task of protecting a child's emotional, physical and spiritual well-being to preserve her innocence.

But it's too late. Lubna and her mother Nahla are tormented by their inability to dream of Ali for different reasons. Lubna is consumed by guilt after breaking the picture frame of her brother, which she did out of jealousy for her mother's attention and love. However, Nahla's mental stability has wavered dramatically since the loss of her son; she is unable to sleep or be intimate with her husband, Khalid, causing a rift between her and the rest of the family. When Nahla discovers that her neighbour Samar has connected with her son through her dreams, she becomes resentful and begins to crack even more. Subsequently Lubna becomes a parental figure in the household, concerned and caring for her mother.

The chaos of the war has also leaked into the neighbouring downstairs apartment of Samar and her husband Ahmad. Their kind and over-sensitive only child, twelve-year-old Khalil, has become violent, lashing out at his mother and throwing a glass in her face. His behaviour is due to his world abruptly becoming smaller – he is confined to playing in the apartment block, with power cuts preventing him from watching television, including his favourite show *Ninja Turtles*. The couple struggle to agree on parenting strategies, as Samar wants to keep her precious child as a baby but Ahmad is keen to treat him like an adult and prepare him for war.

Lubna's friends are all gone, forcing her to befriend her neighbour Khalil, who strangely speaks through his fingers. In the confusion

of their home environment, Lubna and Khalil find comfort in their
new-found friendship. As the two children play on the stairwell
of their apartment block, their understanding of the war, weapons
and the brutal effect it has had on the community, as well as their
own fears, are played out through playful improvised stories. But
Lubna's expectations of her father suddenly shift when she starts
her menstruation. She demands that her father treats her as a
young woman, starting by telling her the truth about her mother's
condition.

As Eid approaches, the parents try to convince their children
that the fireworks (bombs) will end on the first day of Eid. But
as the war intensifies, coming closer to their apartment block,
confessions of acts of defiance against the Israelis and conflictual
desires to remain in the apartment block, result in both families
struggling to keep alive and stay together.

Summary (extract)

A playground. **Lubna** and **Khalil** are playing. They are running
and screaming and jumping around. They are happy. They are
wearing special clothes for Eid. They play for a while, then
suddenly the audience hears an explosion. **Khalil** dies. An eleven-
to twelve-year-old **Lubna**, dressed in her Eid clothes, tells a story
as if it's twenty years later. This speech is performed by **Lubna**
at the end of the play. We realize that her song premonition at
the start of the play has comes to life as she recalls painfully
witnessing the death of her childhood friend.

Lubna   I want to tell you a story. It's actually a poem I tried to write twenty years ago. The poem is about a little boy and a little girl. One day, someone said to the little girl, 'Look, can you see that point where the sky meets the sea. That's where heaven is.' And the little girl loved heaven because it was a really beautiful place and no bad people lived there. And whenever her father told her, 'Ohhhh but you still have a really, really, really long time until you die,' she felt a little bit sad. Because she didn't want to wait a really, really, really long time, because her brother was there and he was playing on his own. So every night she asked God to take her to heaven as soon as possible, and every night she imagined how the angels would come down and fly her up to the sky. And one day the little girl met a little boy, and she said to the little boy, 'Look, can you see that point in the distance where the sky meets the sea. That's where the world ends and heaven starts.' And before she could tell him heaven was a really beautiful place and there were no bad people there, the little boy got angry and said, 'No, that's not true, there's nothing there, and there are bad people everywhere.' The little girl was a bit upset because the little boy didn't believe her, but then she thought he doesn't know what she knows and maybe it's because he's a bit strange and he blows on his fingers when he talks. So the little girl didn't talk to him about heaven again. And one day the little girl and the little boy were playing and the little boy was wearing his flashing trainers and red lights flashed when he ran and the little girl was so happy. Then, suddenly, something happened. The little girl doesn't remember exactly what happened but when she opened her eyes the little boy wasn't moving, and he wasn't blowing on his fingers, and he wasn't screaming.

Nothing was moving except for the flashing red lights in his trainers. The little girl closed her eyes and tried to think of that point where the sky meets the sea. But as soon as she closed her eyes she saw the little boy not moving again. The little girl started walking about looking for someone but there were other little children on the ground and none of them were moving. And she thought maybe the angels will come down now and fly him up to the sky. Then she noticed that the boy's little hand, the hand he blew on when he was speaking, wasn't there. And she didn't want him to be the only boy in the sky without a hand. So she started rushing to find it before the angels came, then the parents of the children arrived. They started hugging them, hugging them really tight, as if they didn't want anyone to take them away. The little girl got scared. She wanted to run as far away and hide in a place where she wouldn't hear the parents screaming. She put her hands over her ears and closed her eyes. But as soon as she shut her eyes she saw the boy. She saw him not blowing on his fingers and not running in his flashing trainers. Lying there, not moving, missing a hand. The girl opened her eyes and started crying and the boy's mother was crying and everyone was hugging the boy's mother and telling her not to worry, that he's happy now, in the sky, happy with God. But the girl thought he's not in the sky, and he's not happy. He's right there, in front of her. She can see him whenever she shuts her eyes. The girl tried to explain to someone that the boy was still there. And the angels hadn't come to fly him up to the sky. But everyone was busy telling the boy's mother how happy he was in the sky and no one would listen to the girl. So the girl decided to keep it secret, and she started sleeping with her eyes open every night so she wouldn't see the little boy. And she started to get black bags under her eyes. And the girl still sleeps with her eyes open, and whenever she sees on TV that someone's died she knows that there's another person sleeping with their eyes open. And the girl knows that one day there will be lots and lots of people who sleep with their eyes open and they will know each other from the black bags under their eyes.

From

TAMAM

by Betty Shamieh

Tamam was presented as part of the Imagine: Iraq Project in 2002 at Cooper Union in New York, curated by Naomi Wallace. The production was directed by José Zayas and performed by the author, Betty Shamieh.

This powerful one-woman play takes its title from the name of the female protagonist, Tamam, which means 'enough'. This compelling and heartfelt story tells the life of Tamam's younger brother who became a suicide bomber. Set during the conflict in Iraq, the act of giving birth to a girl child incites fear in a community that witnesses the daily war against female bodies in war-torn countries. After giving birth to seven girls, Tamam's name was chosen by her parents as a plea for a boy child. The name seemed to have worked because the family were blessed with two boys after Tamam was born. But now there is only one boy left in the family.

Tamam, a young Palestinian woman, is standing alone, on a bare stage. She waits for the audience to take their seats before she tells the story of her deceased younger brother, an aspiring medical student and the apple of her and her parents' eyes, whose death makes her question her views on politics, the cycle of perpetual violence and justice. Tamam bravely unravels the chronological harrowing events which led to his suicide.

Tamam describes her brother (who remains nameless) as a young, loveable, selfless and protective person, who readily put his ambitions on hold, acting against his moral beliefs to financially support the family by building the Israeli settlement in their homeland Gaza. But the hypocrisy of his actions began to chip at him, causing him to rebel in a futile act of protest by throwing rocks at the Israeli guns, which resulted in being placed indefinitely in prison. Within the prison walls, he was subjected to daily torture by the Israeli soldiers and forced to watch the prison guards raping his sister, Tamam. When he is finally released from prison, he is consumed with bitterness, hatred and vengeance.

Over breakfast he hints at his decision to strap a bomb around his waist and blow up an Israeli bus. With conflicted emotions Tamam fails to dissuade him, whispering faintly for him not to go. He leaves the house, never to return, while Tamam is left reconsidering her political views and her faith in Palestinian nationalism begins to temporarily ebb away with the loss of never seeing her brother again.

Summary (extract)

Tamam, a young beautiful Palestinian woman in her mid-twenties, visits her brother in prison and is subjected to being raped by the prison guards in front of her brother.

Tamam   I am a pretty woman.
It's not a compliment, it's not a boast.
It's a fact.
Looks are a commodity, an asset, a possession I happen to possess.
It's why my grandmother said no,
when my sister's brother-in-law asked for my hand.
The family that was good enough
for my plain sister wasn't good enough for me.
I'm a pretty woman.
It's not a boast.
It's a fact.

And I smiled my best smile
when the soldiers opened the gate for me.
Weighed down with baskets of food,
I brought extra,
hoping to create the illusion
that that dirty jail was one place
were there was enough and extra for all
the guards to eat twice.
Otherwise, my brother would get none.
unless there was enough and extra.

They thanked me for the food and they raped me in front of him,
forcing my brother's eyes open so he had to watch.
They wanted to know something
that he preferred not to tell them.
They skewered the support for their argument into my flesh.

I'm told that their torture specialists who study the 'Arab' mind
realized rape would enrage our men.
Enraging a man is the first step on the stairway
that gets him to a place
where he becomes impotent,
helpless.

They not only refer to us as the cockroaches,
they examine us, experiment upon us,
as if we were that predictable, that much the same,
that easy to eradicate.

Their studies show the Arab men value the virtue of their
womenfolk,
Their studies show something within me was supposed to be
inviolate.

Say what you want about Arab men and women
and how we love one another,
There is one thing that's for certain.
There are real repercussions for hurting a woman in my society.
There are repercussions.

When the first hand was laid upon me, we both screamed.
The evolutionary function of a scream is a cry for help,
they tied down the only one who could
so I silenced myself.
That was the only way to tell my brother
I didn't want him to tell.

I flinched when I had to,
but I kept my breathing regular.
My brother tried to look every other way,
but realized I needed him,
to look me in the eyes
and understand.
They thought making us face one another
in our misery would break us.
But we were used to misery.
It's like anything else,
you can build up a tolerance for it.

Someone else told them what they wanted to know,
so they released my brother two weeks later.

That's when he built something
more intricate than the human heart,
hugged it to his chest,
and boarded a bus that was going nowhere and everywhere.

From

Desert Sunrise

by Misha Shulman

Desert Sunrise received its world premiere at Theater for the New City in New York, USA in September 2005. Due to the play's success, it was revived the following year in April 2006. Both productions were directed by the playwright, Misha Shulman, with the following cast: Aubrey Levy (Tsahi), Haythem Noor (Ismail), Alice Borman (Layla), Yifat Sharabi (Soldier 1), Morteza Tavakoli (Soldier 2), Yoel Ben-Simhon (Chorus/Musician) and Bhavani Lee (Dancer). The play was later produced at Northwestern University in Chicago and the Lillian Theatre in Los Angeles.

New-York-based Jerusalem writer Misha Shulman was inspired to write *Desert Sunrise* by several publications, including his father's book *Dark Hope: Working for Peace in Israel and Palestine* (University of Chicago Press, 2007) and his personal trip to the West Bank, where he joined the Israeli-Palestinian peace activist organisation called Ta'ayush. Through this experience, he met people from South Hebron Hills, whose words and experience inspired the play.

Set in a shallow wadi in Israeli-occupied West Bank, *Desert Sunrise* brings together unlikely characters – an Israeli soldier, a Palestinian shepherd, and a young troubled Arab woman – to make a statement about the war, humanity and friendship. Throughout the play a chorus and a musician complement the action and accompany the actors' dances and songs. The play effortlessly combines comedy, music, poetry and dance to tell a tragic, but yet hopeful story.

The action takes place over one night and opens with the gun of Tsahi, an off-duty Israeli soldier, pointed at drum-playing Palestinian shepherd Ismail. In a world where nobody is to be trusted, a lost Tsahi is forced to ask the only person present to steer him in the right direction. The two men, both equally suspicious of each other's motives, enter into a strained conversation based on propaganda-incited generalizations.

It becomes clear that their preconceptions of each other are unfounded and they weaken their guards to proceed into everyday light-hearted conversation and banter.

Tsahi opens up about his recent separation from his girlfriend and Ismail discloses his plans to propose to the love of his life, Layla, on her arrival. While they wait for Layla, Tsahi teaches Ismail how to slow dance like they do in the American movies, so that he can slow dance with Layla. Tsahi encourages Ismail to pretend that he is Layla as they dance, and a rigid Ismail begins to let go of his inhibitions, just as Layla enters. As she watches the two men dancing, a horrified and confused Layla picks up Tsahi's rifle and orders him to let Ismail go.

Layla, who is considered a rebel girl because of her pride, revives the fear and terror of the opening scene, not knowing what or who to trust. Layla reminds Ismail about the recent suffering inflicted on both their families by the Israelis which, unlike Ismail, she cannot forget or forgive as easily.

As we draw deeper into the night, Layla's mental state becomes even more alarming, her dialogue fluctuating between logic and incomprehensible riddles about death. The men hear gunshots and shouting in the near distance and prepare for confrontation. As Ismail fights to get Layla to follow his instructions, Tsahi accidently fires his gun, causing a retaliation of random gunshots with fatal consequences.

Summary (extract)

Layla, a young Arab woman, has just caught her close friend **Ismail** (Palestinian) doing a slow dance with an Israeli soldier **Tsahi**. Completely dumbfounded by their newfound friendship, she holds the men at gunpoint, demanding answers. **Ismail**, who secretly plans to propose to **Layla**, confesses to getting dance lessons from **Tsahi**, imagining he was dancing with **Layla**, to impress her with his new moves. He eventually convinces her to drop the rifle on the ground. But strong-minded **Layla** remains sceptical of **Tsahi** and she enters into a prickly conversation about his motives and the horror that he and his people have inflicted on the Palestinian population.

As the conversation turns to the number of innocent children killed by Israelis versus Palestinians, it triggers a painful memory of the death of a baby whose life was ended as a result of the Israeli soldiers and how **Layla**'s body was also violated.

Layla   I was in the line at the checkpoint. The woman
behind me, her baby was dying. Across the checkpoint was the
ambulance. To save the baby. The soldiers wouldn't let her go
ahead of me. Red, the baby's face, red. I begged them. I begged,
and they laughed. The soldier, he said, 'Kiss me on the lips
and I'll let the baby through.' Off, he ripped it, my hijab, hair
everywhere, woman's hair, my hair. His lips were dry like the
desert. His lips, cigarette breath, my lips wet, I'm wet. My eyes
open, I see the sky. I see the garbage flying. Strange beautiful
birds of the desert. Join them, join them, grow new wings and fly
like a woman, fly. He lets baby go through, to ambulance, too late,
death. Face white, death. Grow new wings and fly …

Fly like a woman! Fly like garbage, right Ismail? You were there.
You saw him kiss me. You saw him rip off my hijab. Everyone
saw! Everyone saw me.

Were you jealous? Is that why you danced with him? Maybe I
should have kissed a female soldier, then at least you wouldn't
bring shame on your family.

Soldier! Kiss Ismail. Ismail wants to be kissed. For him it doesn't
matter. Even if the whole world saw, he could still marry. Because
he's a man. A man!

I will never marry!

I was stained forever by the lips of an Israeli soldier. No Muslim
man could ever erase my mark of shame.

I will have a wedding with eternity. I will be Allah's bride.

From

CHEF

by Sabrina Mahfouz

Produced by P.O.P. *Chef* was first performed at the Underbelly at the Edinburgh Fringe on 31 July 2014. The show then transferred to Soho Theatre in London on 16 June 2015, produced by Just For Laughs Theatricals; this run was followed by a performance at the Latitude Festival on 17 July 2015. All performances were directed by Kirsty Patrick Ward, starring Jade Anouka (Chef). The play won a Fringe First Award, *The Stage* Award for Acting Excellence, as well as being shortlisted for the Carol Tambor Award, Brighton Fringe Award for Excellence and the Holden Street Theatre Award.

British Egyptian playwright Sabrina Mahfouz's one-woman play is sharp, poignant and powerful. As the title suggests, the play centres on the life of a chef who, after achieving the optimal and respected position as Head Chef in a charming bistro restaurant, lands herself in hot water and ends up behind bars, finding sanctuary in a prison kitchen, consumed by dreams of fine cuisine. Inspired by stories viewed from a female perspective, Mahfouz's play focuses on a woman who is physically scarred by disappointments, mistreatments and heartbreaks inflicted by the men in her life, and shows how she discovers self-worth, safety, ambition and a sense of freedom through her passion for food. The drama echoes the energy and unpredictability of life in a working kitchen, as Mahfouz's poetic, lyrical style of writing demands precision, meticulous handling and a playful approach to deal with the nuances, dynamism and subtle political messages. This rise-and-fall story is anchored by the dreams, strength and potential of its protagonist, forcing us to re-examine how we view female prisoners, violence and love.

The action takes place in London, set in a pristinely clean kitchen; the female character named Chef, dressed in a white chef's jacket and jogging pants, appreciates the simplicity of food and begins by writing the name of a dish on the whiteboard. As she narrates the story of her life, we realize that it is far from the name handwritten on the board: 'The Perfect Peach'. From humble beginnings, Chef struggles to make ends meet by making a living from writing about food, while falling deeply and foolishly in love with a drug dealer. Her relationship abruptly comes to an end when she catches the love of her life in bed with another woman. The heartbreak transports her to the kitchen, where for the first time she brings her written recipes to life. Sharing her delicious concoctions secures her a job in a local bistro.

Under the guidance of the head chef, a man with a heart of gold, she learns the fine art of cooking sophisticated cuisines and tasting quality ingredients, perfecting her signature dishes. After four years, her mentor steps down and she succeeds him as Head Chef of the bistro, bursting with aspirations to own her own place. But tragically her past catches up with her, resulting in a prison sentence. Talks turn to missing luxury ingredients and inmate/ kitchen assistant Candice.

As Chef interweaves the mysterious disappearance of self-harmer Candice with her turbulent and painful childhood memories, including one of her father almost strangling her to death, we begin to question her innocence over Candice's sudden bloody departure.

Summary (extract)

In prison, **Chef** is in charge of the prison kitchen and responsible for kitchen staff assistants, including self-harmer **Candice**, who after another suicide attempt has returned from the medical ward to the kitchen on condition that she is kept away from any knife duties. **Chef** has kept her promise, putting **Candice** on mashing duty, but an incident in the kitchen results in **Candice** covered in blood and holding a knife.

NOTE: The author has suggested that the character of Chef can be played by any age and ethnicity; however, for the purpose of this anthology, I have chosen for this piece to be performed by a black female actor in their twenties to correlate with the casting choice of the original production.

Chef   I put her on mashing duty.
Taught her how to make
the best potatoes or turnip or celeriac,
or whatever other root I can convince them to provide,
at just the right consistency using only peelers, mashers
and if cutting was required she passed it on.
I was keeping my promise, my responsibility.
She seemed to like the sounds of the kitchen,
metallic rhythms mixed with her saccharine tones.
When she felt like letting loose
I would come in on the chorus
and Sasha would just nod along.
So we were cool in there,
we're alright, we're fine,
getting through our time one day at a time.
That's what I'd say to her and then –

She pauses.

They said they can't tell us anything.
Not even me.
It's like a huge secret.
I mean we saw her bleeding,

I stepped in her blood,
I was in her blood.
I mean she was just there right there,
I just asked how she was,
then she said all that … stuff.
I'd just said,
hey Candice how are you doing?
She turned on me and usually
I would never be there like that with it in my hand,
usually I'd never be near her with anything
she could use like that,
I signed I promised I knew –
but maybe I was thinking of something else
or maybe I wanted to test her …
No, no that's not what I wanted to do,

definitely not, she was, she is the best one here.
It's. Shit …
The way her wrist just flicked the knife from my hand
so dextrously, so delicately
until she – then it –
the bleeding was so deep I couldn't breathe.
She didn't speak it was so quick,
I screamed they came quick,
I flipped tea towels over the cut,
tripped on the blood,
it stuck to my apron to my nose to my shoes
and I swear she laughed.
I have a bruise now, a big bruise.
They took a picture, said they might need it for future,
for future evidence, in case there was a case,
in case I was involved somehow.
I'm like how,
how could I have been involved
she's my girl, she's my girl
I never did anything!
Yeh, yeh,
that's something we've never heard, Chef.
Don't worry yourself sure it will be fine,
she's unlikely to die, it looked deeper than it was.
This time you probably won't get the blame,
be a shame if you did, we know you liked that kid,
but you know how it goes.
It don't look great you got her blood on your nose
and the knives are locked up, it's only you with the key
and you signed you signed and Dave said
you know she's your responsibility
it's your responsibility –

Thirties

Fabrics

From

I JUST STOPPED BY TO SEE THE MAN

by Stephen Jeffreys

I Just Stopped By To See The Man premiered at the Royal Court
Jerwood Theatre Downstairs, London in November 2000. The
production was directed by Richard Wilson, with the following
cast: Sophie Okonedo (Della), Tommy Hollis (Jesse) and Ciarán
McMenamin (Karl).

Stephen Jeffreys is one of Britain's leading playwrights, the author
of over twenty professionally produced plays. *I Just Stopped By
To See The Man* offers a refreshing look at black appropriation
of music and culture. The play is inspired by the musical genre,
the blues – an art form created by black African Americans such
as Louis Armstrong, Blind Lemon Jefferson, Robert Johnson,
Duke Ellington, Charlie Parker, Dizzy Gillespie and countless
other black artists to confront the forces of racism, poverty and
Jim Crow. Jeffreys juxtaposes the life of a white English musician
motivated by admiration of the blues artists with the life of a black
old-time legendary blues player, to tackle the subject of ownership
and authenticity head-on.

The action takes place in a small shotgun town in Mississippi in
the summer of 1975. Jesse Davidson, a legendary blues artist,
mysteriously died in a car crash with girlfriend Angela fourteen
years ago. His death was questioned by fans and musicians
everywhere, including rock artist Karl from Surrey, England. On
Karl's journey from Memphis to Baton Rough for his next gig,
he stays at a motel in the same area where the allegedly deceased
idol was recently spotted. Led by curiosity and a drug-induced
confidence, he breaks into the home known to belong to Jesse
Davidson.

Jesse's fugitive attractive thirty-four-year-old daughter, Della is
at first shaken by the loud noise of a broken window, but at the
sight of Karl she is quickly put at ease. Unimpressed by Karl,
Della tries her hardest to convince Karl of her father's death. But
die-hard fan Karl proves a hard one to crack, due to his profound

knowledge of the case. Della finally wins Karl over, but as Karl makes his way to leave, he bumps into Jesse at the front door.

Jesse is initially perplexed by Karl – a white, English, chicken-bone-thin guy, who speak with a put-on odd Southern-American accent. When Jesse learns that Karl had never set foot in the South and that his adopted accent came from listening repeatedly to Elmore James albums, he questions Karl's authenticity, connection and ability to sing the blues: 'to sing the blues you have to know the blues'.

Awarded a platinum disc for his version of Jesse's song 'Shotgun Blues' with a considerable amount of royalties, and a following of over 57,000 people who attend his gigs, Karl is adamant to prove that he is not just a one-hit wonder.

Karl eventually discloses the real intention of his visit and proposes that Jesse should join him on stage for a one-night-only 'Back from the Dead' concert, to help save the future of his band and keep him off of drugs. Jesse has not played for fourteen years since the death of his wife, blaming the Devil's music for driving his loved ones away. Della desperately needs her dad to stay in hiding to protect her from the Black Panther party and the police.

Jesse has to decide whether to abandon the only relative in his life or return to the spotlight and be greeted by thousands of fans screaming his name.

Summary (extract)

Thirty-four-year-old ex-university teacher and former member of the Black Panthers **Della** explains why she abandoned her job, betrayed the Black Panther party and now lives in fear for her life.

Della   I did stuff, good stuff. For young black kids.
Consciousness raising, education, making them feel they had some
power. Within the organisation I was trusted as a woman and an
intellectual, which means not trusted at all. Everything had gotten
bureaucratic, a parody of how we started. Decisions were handed
down from on high. Grassroots activity was stamped out. I thought
about quitting but I knew that's what the guy at the top wanted.
So I made it known that I wanted to get involved in something
serious. The word came down that we had a target, a judge. I have
to show up with a gun in my shoulder bag, wait for a guy named
Joshua, hand it over, wait some more and take it away afterwards.
So the killer couldn't be linked to the gun and the gun couldn't be
linked to the killer. I showed up – an underground lot where this
judge parks every Tuesday evening to see his mistress. And there's
Joshua, suit, tie, white shirt, guy looks like he's selling insurance.
He barks at me, takes the gun and says: 'Follow me.' I go: 'No,
the plan is I wait here.' He goes: 'Don't tell me what the plan is,
pussy.' So he's walking fast and I'm running to keep up. And he
goes: 'You watch me do this one, you take the gun and you do
the next one tonight.' Suddenly there's two targets, the judge and
another mark. I'm going: 'What? You pull this stunt now and I
go in with the cops on red alert?' He says: 'This is how we test
people.' He's almost running now, I'm out of breath. There's no
build up. One second this white guy is getting out of a blue Buick,
the next Joshua is charging him, one shot puts him on the floor,
then in close – mouth, neck, stomach five shots. Joshua drops the
gun in my shoulder bag and a car scoops him up. (*Pause.*) I stare
at the dead guy. A long time. I won't say I panicked, it didn't hit
me that way. But what I did was, I emptied the gun out of the
shoulder bag and walked. And I'm in freefall. The cops get lucky,
pull Joshua in at a roadblock, he hasn't made six miles.

He's in the can and the Feds and the brothers are on my tail.

From

HARLEM DUET

by Djanet Sears

Harlem Duet premiered as a Nightwood Theatre production at the Tarragon Extra Space, Toronto, Canada on 24 April 1997. This production was directed by the author, Djanet Sears, with the following cast: Alison Sealy-Smith (Billie), Nigel Shawn Williams (Othello), Barbara Barnes-Hopkins (Magi), Dawn Roach (Amah/ Mona), Jeff Jones (Canada), Lionel Williams (Double Bass), Dough Innes (Cello).

In addition to rave reviews, the play won four 1997 Dora Mavor Moore awards, including Best New Play (Djanet Sears), Best Direction (Djanet Sears), Best Female Performance (Alison Sealy-Smith) and Best Production (Nightwood Theatre). It was remounted at Canadian Stage the following year. In 2006, the Stratford Festival picked it up and *Harlem Duet* became the first play written by a black woman, as well as the first play directed by a black woman, at the festival.

Djanet Sears fearlessly takes on one of the most critically acclaimed and controversial Shakespearean plays, *Othello*, to present a powerful tragicomedy – or as the playwright describes it, 'a rhapsodic Blues tragedy' – about the psychological effects of racial positioning, identity and interracial relationships on the lives and unification of the African American community. *Harlem Duet* spans three monumental periods in Black American history: 1860s during the pre-Emancipation Proclamation America; 1928 during the Harlem Renaissance; and present-day contemporary Harlem, to tell a non-chronological love story which interweaves themes of loyalty, revenge and mental illness.

Inspired by the only role written for a black actor in William Shakespeare's entire repertoire, *Harlem Duet* is a prequel to *Othello*. Although inspired by the character of Othello (controversially historically performed in black face), Sears's play focuses on Othello's first wife, a black woman named Billie, whom he met long before Desdemona. This is Billie's story.

In the scene changes, Sears intersects the most significant
moments in Black American history – including the visit of
Nelson and Winnie Mandela, the famous speech made by Martin
Luther King Jr. on the march on Washington, Marcus Garvey's
call for African American unity, excerpts from the O. J. Simpson
trial – to highlight the historical struggle of being black and living
in a white America. This is the driving force behind the separation
between Billie, an intelligent black woman who embraces
her identity wholeheartedly and seeks strength through her
relationship with the black community, and Othello, who pursues
peace from the burden of racial oppression through the approval
and acceptance of the white community by forming a relationship
with a white woman.

At the core of this drama is the serious and taboo subject of
mental health, a prevalent issue in the black community, as we
witness the lead female character Billie's rapid decline, caused by
the unreciprocated love of the black men in her life, Othello and
her father, which leads to the pertinent question of the roles of
black men in the lives of black women.

Harlem Duet opens with a scene from 1928 in a tiny dressing room
during the Harlem Renaissance. Billie confronts Othello about
his love affair with Mona, a white colleague from the Upper East
Side. Othello confesses his love for Mona to his wife of nine years,
who drops the handkerchief – an heirloom given to her by Othello
on the day he professed his love for her – in disbelief that Othello
has chosen a white woman over her. This moment spills into the
present day with an emotionally broken, sleeping-drug-dependent
Billie asleep in the bedroom of an apartment of a renovated
brownstone on the corner of Malcolm X and Martin Luther King
Boulevard, in New York City. Sister-in-law Amah takes care of
Billie, trying desperately to pull her from depression, encouraging
her to speak with her niece Jenny (Amah's and Billie's brother
Andrew's child) so that they can be a unified family once more, an
offer which Billie constantly feels unready for.

As Amah's personal life moves forward with the news of her
second pregnancy, student graduate Billie remains stuck in the

past, consumed with obsessively analysing her past relationship with Othello and the reasons for his sudden leap from black consciousness activism to assimilation. But when Othello returns to the house to collect his belongings, things take a sudden turn. A painfully heated conversation between the pair about race, in particular white superiority versus blackness, climaxes in an unexpected tender moment of familiarity and love. A passionate kiss from Othello is reciprocated by Billie and the couple make love to each other once more.

An intercom call from Mona instantly shatters the idyllic moment. Othello springs back to his subservient ways and rushes out the house, leaving Billie with even more bitterness and resentment. Billie begins to plot her revenge by poisoning the handkerchief as a gift to Othello. But a fatal mistake causes her plan to backfire.

Summary (extract)

Billie (present day, thirty-seven-year-old black student graduate) is getting her hair greased by **Amah** (sister-in-law). She tries to convince **Amah** of her plans to get her life back on track by returning to school, but subsequently falls back into a reminiscent dialogue about the pain caused by her first love **Othello**.

Billie   Remember when we moved in? The day Nelson and
Winnie came to Harlem, remember? Winnie and Nelson – our
welcoming committee. They'd blocked off the whole of 125th – it
took us 45 minutes to convince the cops to let us through. And me
and you and Othe and Drew went down to hear them speak. And
Drew went off in search of some grits from a street vendor. And
you asked me to hold baby Jenny while you went to the restroom,
when this man came up to us and took our picture. Asked to take
our picture. Jenny in my arms. Othello beside me. 'The perfect
Black family.' That's what he called us. 'The perfect Black
family.'

(*The phone rings.*)

No. Let it ring. I know who it is. I can still feel him – feel when
he's thinking of me. We've spoken … Must be three times, in
the last two months. Something about $500 on my portion of his
American Express card, which they'd cancel if I didn't pay the
bill. Seems I did me some consumer therapy. Last time he called
– mad – to announce that the card had been cancelled by AMEX,
and that he hoped that I was pleased.

(*Beat.*)

And I was. Is that crazy?

I used to pray that he was calling to say he's sorry. To say how
he'd discovered a deep confusion in himself. But now …

I have nothing to say to him. What could I say? Othello, how is
the fairer sexed one you love to dangle from your arm the one you
love for herself and preferred to the deeper sexed one is she softer
does she smell of tea roses and baby powder does she sweat white
musk from between her toes do her thighs touch I am not curious
just want to know do her breasts fill the cup of your hand the lips
of your tongue not too dark you like a little milk with your nipple
don't you no I'm not curious just want to know.

The skin holds everything in. It's the largest organ in the human
body. Slash the skin by my belly and my intestines fall out.

I thought I saw them once, you know – on the subway. I had to
renew my prescription. And I got spot them – him and her. My
chest is pounding. My legs can't move. From the back, I see sharp
barber's lone, separating his tightly coiled hair from the nape of
the skin at the back of his neck. His skin is soft there … and I
have to kick away the memory nudging its way into my brain. My
lips on his neck, gently … holding him … Here, before me – his
woman – all blonde hair and blonde legs. Her weight against his
chest. His arm around her shoulders, his thumb resting on the
gold of her hair. He's proud. You can see he's proud. He isn't
just any Negro. He's special. That's why she's with him. And
she … she … she flaunts. Yes, she flaunts. They are before. I am
behind, stuck there on the platform. My tongue is pushing hard
against the roof of my mouth … trying to hold up my brain, or
something. 'Cause my brain threatens to fall. Fall down through
the roof of my mouth, and be swallowed up. Slowly, slowly, I
press forward, toward them. I'm not aiming for them though. I'm
aiming with them in mind. I'm aiming for beyond the yellow line,
into the tracks. The tunnel all three of us will fall into can be no
worse than the one I'm trapped in now. I walk – no, well hover
really. I'm walking on air. I feel sure of myself for the first time
in weeks. Only to be cut off by a tall grey man in a grey uniform,
who isn't looking where he's going, or maybe I'm not – Maybe he
knew my aim. He looks at me. I think he looks at me. He brushes
past. Then a sound emanating from … from … from my uterus,
slips out of my mouth, shatters the spell. They turn their heads –
the couple. They see me. It isn't even him.

From

A DAY AT THE RACISTS

by Anders Lustgarten

A Day at the Racists was first performed at the Finborough Theatre, London on 2 March 2010. This play was produced by Rogue State Theatre Company in association with Neil McPherson, directed by Ryan McBryde, with the following cast: Thusitha Jayasundera (Gina White/Burka Woman 1), Julian Littman (Peter Case), Sam Swainsbury (Mark Case), Gwilym Lloyd (Tony McDonald/Driver), Vanessa Havell (Labour MP/Polish Lady/Housewife/Journalist), Zaraah Abrahams (Zenobia/Burka Woman 2), Trevor A. Toussaint (Clinton Jones/African Guy) and Nick Holder (Rick Coleman).

A Day at the Racists is a family drama with a difference. At the heart of the story is a political debate about British identity, propaganda and entitlement. Set in one of the most multicultural areas in London during a time of austerity, the play explores how extremist political parties, specifically the British National Party (BNP), are able to succeed in winning the support from opposing party supporters by rebranding their image, propaganda, scaremongering and manipulation.

The Case family have been hit by hard times. Pete Case was a celebrated leading Labour Party organiser who spent years of his life fighting against the British National Party (BNP), but now a struggling decorator unable to compete with the rates of immigrant workers. The current situation of Pete's son Mark, a twenty-three-year-old single parent to a dual heritage daughter, is just as bleak as his father's. Mark suffered a knee injury which hindered his chances of becoming a professional footballer. In place of the once-promising young man with confidence, energy and enthusiasm stands a broken man who finds it difficult to secure housing or employment. Pete desperately wants to help his son, but with exhausted options and feelings of abandonment by the Labour Party, he has nowhere left to turn.

Newly appointed BNP candidate Gina White, a mixed race white-Pakistani, becomes the answer to Pete's problems. Gina is a formidable woman with an unyielding patriotism which drives her vision for a modern take on the BNP. Gina is determined to prove her place in the British National Party against the wishes of the party's long-standing regional local organizer, Tony McDonald. McDonald is an out-and-out racist who openly shares his disapproval of her appointment and uses any opportunity to disclose his desire for a white-only Britain.

Pete's previous experience in politics is not lost on Gina, who is certain that she will be able to make a success of her campaign with him on side. All she needs to do is convert him. She astutely identifies Pete's vulnerability and desperation to support his son and relentlessly indulges him in emotional brainwashing, together with kind gestures including accommodation for his son and granddaughter and a secure job as the organizer of the election campaign. Pete succumbs to Gina's bribery.

Things take a turn for the worse when Mark, who is attracted to African-Caribbean women, sees his daughter's face on a BNP poster. He confronts his dad and discovers the truth about Pete's new occupation. The relationship between father and son instantly fractures, leaving Pete ostracized from his son and granddaughter's life.

Summary (extract)

Gina (a young, well-dressed mixed race white-Pakistani woman) is adamant to succeed in her plans to convince **Pete**, a former leading Labour Party organizer, to join the British National Party. But after a recent confrontation with racist local organizer, **Tony McDonald**, who outwardly racially abuses **Gina** and unashamedly voices his longing for an all-white Britain, **Pete** begins to have second thoughts. **Gina** detects that **Pete** is backing away from the idea and, in **Tony McDonald**'s absence, attempts to sell him her ideology of a new modern BNP.

Gina   People like him are a dying breed. I'm the future. *I* am.

[...]

Look at me, is that what you're gonna say? Who's the racist now, Pete? 'You're a Paki, you stay with the other Pakis.'

[...]

I thought this country was about freedom, where's the freedom in that? Fuck any system that says my dad can come over here and keep his disgusting Paki ways –

[...]

That is what they are, Pete! What kind of freedom says my Dad can marry me off to some obese stinking fifty-year-old peasant from his village who signs his name with his thumbprint and tries to stick his cock up my arse on the wedding night? And then my white mother and all her kind tell me it's 'my culture' and I should be *grateful* to have it, because she's too fucking scared and lost and weak to know what's hers and so in her mind she's *brave* for sucking my dad's dick and getting his passport because she didn't have to, she could've married that ginger IT engineer from Huddersfield and never had the neighbours whispering. Fuck all that.

[...]

Don't go. What made you come in? Once you saw Mr Knuckle-dragger there, you could have slipped back out the way you came. What made you stay?

[...]

(*Beat.*) There is a great mass of humanity out there, lost and lonely and afraid, that we can reach. Help me find what the people need and want and dream of. Give them a little of what's been stolen from them and they will be ours forever.

[...]

I can make a real difference in people's lives. [...] But I need an organiser. [...] A man with experience. [...] A man with passion and intelligence, whose passion and intelligence are being criminally wasted as of now.

[...]

A man who wants to make a difference in other people's lives, and his own.

From

THE HUSBANDS

by Sharmila Chauhan

The Husbands was co-produced by Kali Theatre and Pentabus
Theatre Company. The play premiered at The Drum in Plymouth,
England on 12 February 2014, followed by a regional tour. It
was directed by the Artistic Director of Kali Theatre Company,
Janet Steel, with the following cast: Syreeta Kumar (Aya), Rhik
Samadder (Sem), Mark Theodore (Omar) and Phillip Edgerley
(Jerome).

Chauhan's play boldly catapults audiences into an imaginary
world where the gender roles are reversed. It is set in modern rural
India where women are valued, respected, educated and in charge.
The action takes place in a fictional matriarchal community called
Shaktipur, located in Kerala, South India, in a gated community
set up over fifty years ago to combat the decreasing numbers of
girls in India as a result of female foeticide, infanticide, abduction
and death. In Shaktipur, women are revered, the community
worships female Hindu goddesses, and female residents are
encouraged to live a life of polyandry to increase the number of
girls born in order to create a healthy balance.

The story follows the life a strong, intelligent, attractive woman
called Aya, the newly appointed leader of this gated community.
Strong-minded Aya has no intention of adhering to all the
traditions of Shaktipur. She has her mind set on growing the
empire, expanding Shaktipur to the city to increase support and
freedom for women throughout India.

Aya is happily married to two husbands: Sem and Omar. The
play begins on the morning of Aya's third wedding to a man from
Mumbai, as the husbands prepare the food for the celebration.
Sem is excited about the prospect of the third husband providing
the family with a child. But the anticipation of another husband
winning Aya's affection leaves Omar with feelings of jealousy
and insecurity as he desperately desires to win Aya's heart and
father Aya's children. When an unexpected and unwanted stranger

appears at the house, Aya's secrets gradually unfold and her great plans for the future become less obtainable.

The Husbands is a story of love, jealousy and freedom. Through the play Chauhan questions the role of women in society in relation to freedom, sexuality, duty, leadership and motherhood, forcing us to consider if woman have the right to choose when it comes to motherhood.

Summary (extract)

Aya, an Indian woman in her mid-thirties, is described as enigmatic, intelligent and sensual. **Aya**'s secret pregnancy is exposed to her husbands by her British lover, **Jerome**. The husbands are ecstatic at the prospect of being fathers, but **Aya** is conflicted. Her plans to marry her third husband and travel to Mumbai to abort the baby in order to start the expansion of Shaktipur are jeopardized. If she is unable to convince her husbands to lie about her pregnancy to her fiancé and wedding guests, she will have to wait three years to marry. Jerome wants her to leave Shaktipur and live with him in England, where she can have 'freedom'. Her husbands, **Sem** and **Omar**, want **Aya** to stay loyal to them and the traditions and people of Shaktipur. But **Aya** has no desire to be a mother and sacrifice everything she has built.

Aya   Oh Sem …
A new life?
Don't you see …
This new life
It will be your new life (*Pause … then very quiet.*)
And the very end of mine …

(*Long silence.*)

Of everything I believe in
Everything I have worked for
(*to OMAR*)
Please, try to understand
This child doesn't belong here …

(*Ignoring him and touching her stomach.*)
I can feel it
A tiny life flickering inside
Like a candle in the monsoon night
It's growing already … Taking parts of me
Piecing it all together … By itself
In the morning
It stirs up my insides
Bringing to my lips
The acid regurgitation
Of my dreams
Already it tells me …
Mother, you belong to me
…
One month and already this?
…
Sem, don't you see?
It is taking me somewhere I do not want to go
By the hand into the darkness
Calling me … But …

(*beat*)

I don't want to be called …
Mother
It says I'm coming …

(**Aya** *turns away. Roll of thunder closer.*)

I disappoint you
I disappoint myself
…

I do not want a child and then have to make allowances for it
Or not make allowances and let the guilt swallow me whole
Can't you see, it will tear us apart?

…

(*Shaking her head.*) For you I would do anything.
But this …
Once it's here I won't be able to turn away from it.
Can't you see that?

…

I love you Omar, but it doesn't mean I want to be a mother to your child.

From

A CANADIAN MONSOON

by Sheila James

Produced by the Company of Sirens, *A Canadian Monsoon*
received its first professional production in June 1996 at the
Theatre Passe Muraille Main Space, directed by Sharon Fernandez,
with the following cast: Bina Sharif, Catherine McNally, Gail
Maurice, Sharon Lewis, Sonia Dhillon and Sean Tagore.

A Canadian Monsoon was the first Indo-Canadian play to
receive such critical acclaim. Sheila James's witty, poignant and
hard-hitting play boldly explores the lives of women, looking at
gender roles, motherhood, violence and culture. Set in Canada,
James uses the metaphor of the monsoon – a rainy season in India
which can sometimes lead to the destruction of bridges, houses
and roads, as well as nourish crops and renew land – to symbolize
the Indian traditions and cultural practices being wiped out by
the next generation of the Isaac family. The setting of the play
alternates between the Isaac household and Thomas and Gina's
clinic. James also includes surreal episodes which complement but
also occur in isolation to the main story to expose the misogynistic
attitudes and violence to women's bodies. Some include abortion
scenes, or doctors discussing the sex of the embryo to decide
whether it is worth keeping or throwing away.

The action takes place on the day of Sunita's thirty-third birthday.
Sunita's mother Aruna, a recent widow, speaks to her late
husband's photograph, expressing her fears of never experiencing
the joys of being a grandmother. Raised as a village girl of
humble beginnings, she acquired her wealth and status through
her husband, who brought her to Canada twenty-five years ago.
The move enabled her to provide a better life for her children, but
now they are fully grown adults with no children of their own.
Consumed by desperation, outspoken Aruna preoccupies her time
by enforcing her wishes for grandchildren on a daily basis.

Meanwhile, at the clinic Aruna's daughter, Sunita has her hands
full making out with Gina on the office desk. Gina wants them to

take their relationship to the next stage by moving in together. But Sunita feels her obligations should be with her mother.

Aruna's son Thomas is the golden boy of the family, a medical doctor who proves to be more accepting of cultural traditions. He agreed to an arranged marriage with a young woman named Shanta who was selected by his mother and brought from India to Canada. Shanta gets pregnant soon after they wed, which ends in a still birth. The incident was never spoken about, and the couple instead focus their energy on having another child. But Thomas has been straying from home, having an affair with his mentally unstable patient, Carolyn.

When a number of strange anonymous gifts, in the form of brown baby dolls in nappies, are delivered to the clinic, Gina finds out that they belong to Shanta, who is now pregnant for the second time. The only problem is that Shanta does not want to keep the baby, but feels she has no choice. Shanta admits to knowing about Gina and Sunita's lesbian relationship and considers having the baby to distract Aruna from finding out about her daughter's secret homosexual love affair.

But regardless of Shanta's efforts, the truth about Sunita's sexuality is revealed to Aruna. As her children pull further away from cultural norms and expectations, will Aruna disown her only daughter, or will the family be able to survive the monsoon and stay together?

Summary (extract)

Sunita (thirty-three-year-old Indo-Canadian) is clearing up the plates and putting things away. She is alone. She opens up about her job as an abortion specialist, and her experience both as a patient and a doctor.

Sunita   (*Lights dim and focus on* **Sunita**. *She starts clearing up the plates, putting things away.*) Never in daylight, in front of an appreciative audience, but after hours, in back rooms and deserted alleys. I move from operating table to kitchen counter, human blood, animal blood, on my clothes, on my hands.

I woke up in a crimson pool; scared, was it me. But then, in half relief and half fear, I realized it was the blood of women I knew. Mummy, Shanta … Gina. They were crying … blood pouring out from between their legs. I tried to find napkins, tampons, diapers, anything to stop the bleeding. I found a box of pads, reached inside, only to pull out a handful of condoms. But there were little holes in the tips, dripping with semen and now a pregnancy epidemic had broken out … in India, Pakistan, Bangladesh, Nepal, Sri Lanka. Girls and women, twelve to sixty years of age were pregnant and knocking on my door.

'Please Doctor Ji, I am an old woman, I have already ten children to feed. I can not bear another.'

'Amma, my daughter has been raped, if she has this child she'll be ruined. No man will marry her.'

'No, Doctor Amma, see me, my husband is impotent. If he finds I'm pregnant he'll know I've been unfaithful, he'll kill me, I swear he'll kill me.'

And as I start to operate, one after the other, women start going into labor. It's as if time doesn't exist. It's lightning! Children are bursting from wombs. Some spring into life, healthy and vibrant, rosy red cheeks on fairer skin, but others, the dark ones, are all abnormal, some born with several heads, animal limbs, and others, oh god. Others born with big bellies ready to give birth themselves. It's too much. They surround me with their cries, their pleas, and blood just keeps pouring off the tables onto the floor, red rain into red rivers, overflowing into the fields, into the streets. When I woke up, my body was damp with sweat and menstrual blood began a sluggish flow between my legs. Ah, the monthly reminder that I can. Still.

(*Lights down.*)

From

RICE BOY

by Sunil Kuruvilla

Rice Boy received its world premiere at the Yale Repertory
Theatre, New Haven, Connecticut, America in October 2000,
directed by Liz Diamond with the following cast: Wayne
Kasserman (Tommy), Angel Desai (Tina), Sean T. Krishnan
(Father), Sanjiv Jhaveri (Uncle), Shaheen Vaaz (Auntie), Yolande
Bavan (Granny), Anita Gandhi (Servant Girl/Fish Seller/Clerk),
Ajay Naidu (Umbrella Man/Nut Seller) and Colin Lane (Mr
Harris/Mennonite Farmer). The play received a West Coast
premiere at the Mark Taper Forum, Los Angeles, California in
April 2001, directed by Chay Yew, and premiered in Canada at
the Canadian Stage Company, Toronto, Ontario in March 2003,
directed by Micheline Chevrier.

Set in 1975, *Rice Boy* alternates between Kottayam in South India
during the summer and six months later in Kitchener, Ontario
in the winter. The title and overarching theme of the play pays
homage to a Hindu cultural practice whereby the women would
grind the rice and use the powder created to design elaborate
kolams (patterns) on their front porch that disappear over a very
short period of time, reinforcing the idea of creation, endings
and letting go. This theme of loss is a central theme of the play,
explored through its protagonist, twelve-year-old Tommy, who
returns to India with his father for the first time since the tragic
death of his mother, who drowned in a river ten years prior.
Rice Boy deals with themes of cultural displacement, memories,
identity and love, as each character in the play struggles to deal
with a transitional moment in their lives.

Twelve-year-old Tommy is accustomed to life in Canada,
but everything changes during the summer of 1975 when he
accompanies his father to his native birthplace in India to learn the
importance of his cultural heritage and attend his sixteen-year-old
cousin Tina's arranged marriage to a man she has never met. But
not long after their arrival, his father quickly realizes that India

is far removed from the nostalgic images painted in his mind and an unforeseen situation leaves Tommy never wanting to return to India ever again.

The play opens with Tina, a homebound paraplegic girl, practising her Kalams on the front porch as she prepares for the conventional marital duties of a wife under the watchful eye of her grandmother and mother. Tina's mother and father, referred to in the play as Auntie and Uncle, have other reasons for wanting Tina to perfect her duties. Barely holding on to a loveless marriage, both have qualified reasons to distrust the other and unanimously agree to separate after Tina's wedding.

As Tommy sits in a tree distancing himself from an unfamiliar environment, yearning for the modern city life, toilets and toilet paper, his father's experience is overshadowed by the tragic event which took place a decade ago, resulting in the death of his wife who mysteriously drowned in the river behind the family house, her body never discovered. Consumed by grief and unable to move on, Tommy's father has never been the same since her disappearance. Fired from his post as a maths professor, he moved between retail and restaurant jobs, unable to sustain a position for long. In India, he spends the days throwing rocks into the river, pondering the whereabouts of his missing wife.

As the play develops, Tommy builds a strong bond with his cousin Tina and discovers that her desire for marriage is enraptured desperation to see the world beyond the front porch of the family home. Tommy sneaks his cousin into the city and they both get an opportunity to see India with new eyes.

A night before the wedding, Tommy encourages his cousin to take one last adventure with him. She reluctantly agrees but insists on making her own way home. On the morning of the wedding, Tina still has not returned. Her unexplained disappearance chimes with that of his mother's, leaving Tommy guilt-stricken and confused. He slowly realizes that he is neither Indian nor Canadian. His father lets go of the thought of his wife returning and he and Tommy find comfort in each other.

Summary (extract)

Auntie (thirty-five-year-old woman) is on the front porch with her daughter **Tina**. **Auntie** opens up about her marriage and reason for believing that her husband is being unfaithful.

Auntie   Long time ago. Before you were born. I would take lunch to your father at the talcum factory. One day I went but he wasn't there. The men said he had to go for a meeting so I left the tifin. The next day, same thing. What meeting? I went to the perfume store to buy more soap and I saw him rush by the window. So fast, just by himself. He crossed the street and went into the cinema. I bought a ticket to surprise him. Up and down the aisle I walked, looking, trying to find him. I went to the balcony. He was there sitting with his accountant. She was an old woman, so dark, so ugly. Yes, she was taller than me but I'm a short thing. So loud it was, people shouting at the movie but the two of them were just there, not even talking. And they were having ice cream. Like a little boy. Your father doesn't take ice cream! I went straight to the woman's house and told her husband. That night he broke her arm – the neighbours had to run for the police. The woman wouldn't say what happened but her husband did. Your father cried and told me sorry but I just laughed at him – he could only get an old woman. Ann was her name. I knew because they weren't talking. And the ice cream. I am a very smart woman. You father doesn't rush, always keeps me waiting.

From

9 PARTS OF DESIRE

by Heather Raffo

9 Parts of Desire was originally produced by Erich Jungwirth,
Voice Chair Productions; Richard Jordan, Richard Jordan
Productions, Ltd. It received its world premiere in August 2003 at
the Traverse Theatre, Edinburgh, Scotland, written and performed
by the author Heather Raffo and directed by Eva Breneman.
In September 2003, the play transferred to the Bush Theatre in
London. In 2004, *9 Parts of Desire* had its New York premiere
at the Manhattan Ensemble Theatre, performed by the author
Heather Raffo and directed by Joanna Settle.

Iraqi-American playwright, Heather Raffo's poignant one-woman
play about Iraqi women during the first and second Gulf Wars and
American occupation was inspired by the author's trip to Baghdad
in 1993. There she visited the Saddam Art Center and viewed
a painting titled 'Savagery', depicting a naked woman holding
onto a barren tree, head hanging low with a bright light behind
her. Both the picture and the life of the much-adored female artist
Layla Al-Attar (who was killed by an American air raid in 1993)
are featured heavily in her play. In addition, Raffo spoke with
a wide range of Iraqi women over the course of ten years; the
information gathered informed the narrative of the play's nine
female characters.

Heather Raffo's play shares the same title as Geraldine Brooks's
book, which also centres on Islamic women. The book inspired
Raffo to create a ninety-minute play. Moreover, the title refers to a
quote by the founder of the Shiite sect of Islam, Ali ibn Abi Talib,
who believes 'Almighty God created sexual desire in ten parts;
then he gave nine parts to women and one to men'. Raffo's play
portrays nine Iraqi women located in different parts of the world,
who all speak candidly about their sexual desires and longing for
peace, justice and freedom. *9 Parts of Desire* paints an honest
and disturbing account of the atrocities carried out under Saddam
Hussein's regime, leaving no stone unturned as the women unveil

the brutality of war inflicted on their bodies, psyches and loved ones.

At the start of the play, the actor uses an abaya (a traditional black robe-like garment which alternates between being worn and used as a prop, depending on the character) together with a series of exceptionally well-written monologues to represent the lives of the nine very different contemporary Iraqi women. Each woman portrays a different political view. The main speaker in the play, Layal, an artist renowned for painting nude self-portraits, is favoured by the regime due to painting pictures of Saddam. However, she still cannot escape the abuse, being forced to give sexual favours to Saddam's son and witness the horrifying torture of her friend, who was fed to dogs. A nine-year-old girl, who after the American soldiers visited her school spends her days at home dancing to music by her favourite American boyband NSYNC, recalls the death of her grandparents and brags about her ability to distinguish types of weapons based on the sound they make when fired. But when we are introduced to the American character who watches the atrocities from her living room in the States, begging for America to stop and acknowledge the deaths and lives affected by the war, we begin to question our moral compass and are forced to re-examine the actions taken by the West.

Summary (extract)

Layal is the curator of the Saddam Art Center. She wears the abaya loosely hanging off her shoulders like a dressing gown or painting smock. She is sexy and elegant, a resilient and fragile woman, a daredevil with a killer smile. **Layal** now lives at her sister's house, after her own house was bombed by 'Bush's war', she lost everything including the paintings for her new exhibition. She talks metaphorically about love for Iraq from America, and why they could never love Iraq like an Iraqi woman.

NOTE: No age is specified by the author for this role.

Layal   Maybe they think I am dangerous?

Maybe I am, I am attached like I will die if I leave.
I think you're dangerous.
Americans they are not so attached this way
they feel so free, even to be alone.
I am afraid to be alone.
I don't want freedom – to be alone?
I don't care for it, I like protection
all I want is to feel it, love –

I am crazy for it,
I am hungry every morning like I have never eaten before,
and there is never enough to feed me
so when I find more
I risk everything for it
oblivion even, I don't care
I submit completely.
And still I am empty
I never feel worth
because I shouldn't be so hungry
because others are not so hungry
or they can control it – but I cannot myself
I cannot keep my mind from flesh
I tell you, even when I fell in love
not with my husband
after I was married
really I fell in love
it humiliated me
to finally see
how much of myself I could never be
and I hated it
not to be full
not to feel whole
it's the worst feeling this occupation
to inhabit your body but not to be able to live in it.

So I had an affair! (*She laughs.*)
I let myself love him –

we were just a boy and a girl in art school
painting, drawing, very expressive
you can't imagine the freedoms
we had teachers from all over the world coming to Baghdad
I was very messy
and when my husband found out
he shot me.

I thought I was dead

And even in the emergency room I was saying,
'No it was me,
with the gun, it was me, it was an accident.'
We never spoke about it
but he never stopped me from having an affair again!

I think
most women must be so hungry
because they love with such a sacrifice
an aching
but I tell you,
when you're this way
so attached
always loving like you will die without something –
you love like an Iraqi woman! (*Laughing.*) Shaharazard!
Oh Americans, they have this passion to save everything
because they have such a big footprint, they feel guilty.
They are a very handsome teenager
so tall and strong
passionate, selfish, charming
but they don't think.

You have
our war now
inside you, like a burden, like an orphan
with freedom, intelligence, all opportunity and choice
yet we tether you to something so old you cannot see it –
we have you chained
to the desert
to your blood

you carry it in you – it's lifetimes
and you fight your war to unchain yourself
you come back
you feel at home here
maybe different
maybe more than in your country-
but you hate us, too
because you cannot breathe
because we are not free –
you are not free, you love too much.
It's the same, all, anywhere you live
if you love like an Iraqi woman
if you love like you cannot breathe.

From

THE BELOVED

by Amir Nizar Zuabi

The Beloved was first produced by the Palestinian theatre company ShiberHur in a Young Vic production co-produced with the Bush Theatre and KVS Brussels on 21 May 2012. This production was directed by the author, Amir Nizar Zuabi, with the following cast: Sivan Sasson (Wife), Jonatan Bukshpan (Young Son), Makram J Khoury (Abraham), Rami Heuberger (Son), Rivka Neumann (Mother), Taher Najib (Wise Ram) and Samaa Wakeem (Young Lamb).

Amir Nizar Zuabi rehashes the biblical story of Abraham and Isaac to create a harrowing family drama about human sacrifice, faith and love. The story of Abraham is well known and celebrated in three religious denominations, namely Islam, Christianity and Judaism, used as a significant example of faith. God tested Abraham's devotion to him by asking for the ultimate sacrifice, his own flesh and blood – his son. Abraham passed the test because he was prepared to sacrifice his only son, demonstrating his complete submission and devotion to God.

In *The Beloved*, Zuabi revolutionizes the story of Abraham by adopting magical realism and setting the play against the backdrop of the conflict in the Middle East. Set in a home located near the border at time of war, destruction and atrocity, we are forced to question the act of human sacrifice in the name of religion and authority, as well as the psychological impact it has on the next generation.

In Zuabi's beautifully crafted abstract story, the sacrificial lamb is personified to form the character of Young Lamb, who not only speaks but whose piercing high-pitched bleat replaces the harrowing cry of the son, mother, Wise Ram (who witnesses the attempted murder) and even God. The bleating sound is a repetitive noise throughout the piece, allocated at the optimal moments; it is this sound which stops Abraham from killing his son with a knife in the mountains. Unlike the biblical versions, the play's protagonist is Abraham's son, who, after his visit to the mountains with his father, returns home without any obvious physical scars but is mentally damaged. The story follows his turbulent journey from a ten-year-old child post-mountain trip and then again several years later as a thirty-year-old husband, to show the lasting impacts of emotional trauma caused by witnessing his dad trying to kill him with a knife – an event which has costly consequences on the son's relationship with his parents and his wife.

The play opens with the Son and Abraham returning to their humble abode several days after their unannounced trip to the mountains, confronted by a distressed Mother. The ten-year-old Son is forbidden to speak about his experience in the mountains, which causes his mother to become even more anxious, as she proceeds to strip her son to his underpants searching for evidence of mistreatment. The reason for the Mother's erratic behaviour becomes clear when we learn about her first-born son, who under the guidance of Abraham was taken by the army and died at war – a memory that has cast a grey cloud over the marriage ever since. The couple constantly fight about their only living son. Abraham wants to toughen his son to prepare him for fighting in the war, in contrast to the Mother, who wants to preserve his innocence and keep him as far away from the war as humanly possible.

As the play develops, the Son's emotional state deteriorates rapidly; he begins to reject the lamb stew that he loved so much and has a complete mental breakdown at the dinner table. This outburst leads to the Mother and Son escaping from the house without Abraham's knowledge.

Twenty years later, the Son is now a thirty-year-old butcher happily married to his loving Wife. But things take a drastic turn when the Wife announces that she is pregnant with a boy. The Son acts out of trauma-induced rage and violently assaults his wife, claiming to be inadequate to be a father to a son and intentionally causes her to have a miscarriage.The Wife leaves and the Mother returns to care for her mentally unstable son. But seven years later the Wife returns unexpectedly to give the Son the biggest ultimatum of his life. But will the son be courageous enough to return to the Moriah mountains, the place where his life transformed forever, to take the life of his controlling father in order to regain control of his own life, repair his marriage and fulfil his wife's desires of procreating new life?

Summary (extract)

At this point of the play, the **Wife** is thirty-seven years old. After spending the entire night patrolling around the house trying to find the courage to confront her husband after the vicious attack which caused the miscarriage, she enters the house. She is greeted by the **Son**'s protective **Mother**, who refuses to leave the married couple alone for fear that his **Wife** might cause him harm. As they sit awkwardly around the dinner table eating stew and drinking milk, the **Wife** breaks the silence and talks directly to her husband for the first time in seven years, with one final request.

Wife   Seven years I spent my nights wanting to kill you, then kill
the memory of you and of my dead son and I couldn't.
Spent my nights imagining how I put my hand in your blood,
up to the elbow and then spent the nights biting my hand till it
bleeds so I don't scream my pain.
It's very good the stew.
Then spent my nights staring at the ceiling hoping it will
cave in on me, hoping that one second between 3:46
and 3:47 in the morning
I will hear a crack and the whole thing will crash down,
suffocating me in a mix of concrete, metal.
Seven years all I wanted was to kill then die,
Kill you, then die.
Two and a half thousand days
and then the pain became comfortable.
It mixed with the water I drank and the salt on my bread –
until one day
I looked through the window and in the middle of the street
there was a lamb, a small lamb,
standing there eating the flowers growing on the
roundabout,
cars rushing all around him,
but him calm, so calm, chewing flowers.
He looked at me, big black eyes
and I knew why he was there in the middle of traffic.
Two and a half thousand days.
That's how long it took me to forgive you.
And then at once all I wanted was
to see you, touch you, smell you.
I wanted to be home with my husband.

From

OH MY SWEET LAND

A Love Story From Syria

by Amir Nizar Zuabi

Oh My Sweet Land received its world premiere at Théâtre de
Vidy-Lausanne, Switzerland on 12 November 2013. This production
was subsequently followed by a UK premiere at the Young Vic
Theatre on 4 April 2014. The play was written and directed by Amir
Nizar Zuabi, and conceived and performed by Corinne Jaber.

Amir Nizar Zuabi's immensely powerful one-woman play is based
on the stories he encountered at the Syrian refugee camps in Jordan.
Love stories take on different meanings from play to play, and
although this play is considered a love story, the plot itself is much
broader than two people falling in love and finding happiness,
which is sadly not the fairy-tale ending for the protagonist. Instead
the main message is about humanity, our attitude towards the
people of Syria and the many refugees around the world. Zuabi
brilliantly captures the spirit of the refugees and the war-inflicted
cities that they live in, using a poetic language that explodes off the
written page with urgency, leaving no place to hide.

Oh My Sweet Land is centred on the life of an unnamed female
character who addresses the audience from her kitchen in Paris
as she makes the classic Syrian dish called Kubah and recalls
her search to find the love of her life and reconnect with her
father's homeland. The play opens with the character sharing an
embarrassing childhood memory of living in Munich (Germany)
aged nine years old, despising all things Syrian, starting with
her Syrian grandmother, Teta Amina, who came to stay with
them. Ashamed of the appearance, attire and smell of her Kubah-
cooking grandmother, the character would cringe at anyone's
recognition of her likeness to her Syrian attributes, the Syrian dish
Kubah and Arabs.

This all changes when she meets and falls in love with an exiled
Damascene medical worker, Ashraf, a man who looks just like

her father. Ashraf carries the guilt after escaping the horrors of his war-torn homeland, leaving behind his friends and relatives. Over the course of three months, she helps him organize the escape of fellow Syrians via Skype from the comfort of her home, and a love affair blossoms between them.

One morning she wakes up to find that Ashraf is missing. Confused by his sudden disappearance, she sets off on a lengthy and dangerous journey through Lebanon, Jordan and Syria to find him. With a picture of Ashraf she seeks the help of refugees to locate his whereabouts, but quickly discovers that everyone has a story of displacement and loss. We follow her journey, which inevitably becomes a window into the devastation, pain and the inerasable sightings of thousands of refugees whose homes, land and hearts are left with abundant gaping holes caused by the civil war.

On her journey she is captured and imprisoned. After a week she is released from prison and Ashraf gets her out of Syria, but not before she has the chance to reunite with the love of her life with new eyes. Ashraf looks different, more comfortable than she has ever known him to look. She boards the plane to return home alone, filled with nostalgic memories of her father. The experience of Syria has given her a deeper understanding of Ashraf, her father and the part of her that she tried so desperately to reject.

Summary (extract)

The unnamed lead character, a dual heritage German-Syrian woman, is a famous actress. On her search to find her lover **Ashraf** who disappeared in the middle of the night, she travels to Zahlé, gives a speech at a demonstration and ends up in prison. In this extract she recalls her experience of being detained for three months.

NOTE: The author of the play has set no specific age for this character. For the purpose of this anthology I would recommend an actor 30+ years.

When I got home the Mukhabrat were waiting for me outside …
Driving to the station one of them asked for my autograph
One we got inside
I was stripped naked and beaten
I was no longer the famous actor
For three days I was blindfolded
locked in a cell one and a half metres by two
with thirteen others
That's forty-five square centimetres per person
That's the size of this napkin
I was there for three days before I was taken
to meet my interrogator
It turned out he was critical of my politics
but far more critical of my acting
I got to hear I am a shitty actor with a shitty presence and a shitty
voice
that I'm the shittiest actor in Syria
I don't know which hurt more
his punches to my face or his artistic criticism
then he kicks me in the face
I hear a strange sound
like styrofoam breaking
I think it's my nose breaking but it could be my cheekbone as my
head hits the floor
Then I see them,
black pointy leather shoes
I noticed them in the window of a shoe shop
In Shkib Arslan Street last week
They were in a sale
I went in but they didn't have my size
I'm lying on the floor
I can see blood on the floor
It's my blood, it's coming from my nose
forming a small pool in front of my face
The tip of his shoe is in the blood
I imagine how my blood is seeping into his shoe
wet red socks
Suddenly I feel sorry for him

I know that's crazy but it's the truth
and I know that's my only chance
my only chance to save my life
It's a shame to ruin your new shoes in my blood, I say
He's confused
I grab my chance
You got the last pair of size forty-fives
I wanted them but you got the last pair, didn't you?
You got them in the sale or did you pay full price?
In the sale, he says
They're nice, I say as I sit up
They look nice on you, they suit you,
yes, but you shouldn't wear them to work
they're too nice to ruin
He looks at his shoes and smiles to himself
I will live
I'm beaten a bit more but know it's only for protocol
He asks me to sign a blank piece of paper
my confession
We want your autograph, nothing more, he says smiling
An autograph from the great Syrian actor
Sign it
I'm returned to the cell
A week later I'm released
Ashraf gets me out of Syria
He himself took Suryya and Ream and went to Jordan
He wants to be close to Taffas, close to Syria
I want to be as far away as possible from Syria
and its black pointy shoes

From

WEDDING DAY AT THE CRO-MAGNONS

by Wajdi Mouawad

translated by Shelley Tepperman

Wedding Day at the Cro-Magnons was first performed at the
Mercury Theatre, Colchester as a co-production with Dialogue
Productions in association with Soho Theatre, on 26 March
2008. This production was directed by Patricia Benecke with
the following cast: Celia Meiras (Nelly), Patrick Driver (Neyif),
Karina Fernandez (Souhayla), Mark Field (Neel), Jeremy Killick
(Gentleman) and Beverley Klein (Nazha).

Wedding Day at the Cro-Magnons is the British debut of Wajdi
Mouawad, a Lebanese writer now based in Canada. The play is
billed as an 'anarchic comedy', set in a fictional world against
the backdrop of war, where nothing seems to go right. It's the
morning of Nelly's wedding day and as bombs fall from the sky,
the narcoleptic bride-to-be remains off-stage drifting in and out of
slumber, while the family prepare the wedding feast – an almost
impossible task. The mother is keen to provide a delicious banquet
to impress the wedding guests, but when her son gets fobbed off
by the Armenian shopkeeper returning home to the Cro-Magnon
family with wet lettuce, while the dad struggles to pull the sheep
which the butcher had no time to slaughter, she is left holding a
handful of soggy potatoes from the kitchen pondering her options.
Luckily, next door neighbour Souhayla saves the day by arriving
with an array of appetizing Lebanese dishes. In between sleeps,
an impatient and excitable Nelly calls out to enquire if it's time to
leave for Berdawnay and about the whereabouts of her wedding
dress.

But as the story unfolds we realize that the wedding food is the
least of the family's worries. Unbeknownst to Nelly, her family
fabricated the story about her European fiancé to lift the spirit
of the house at a time of war, but are now unsure how to break
the news to Nelly and the expected wedding party. Against all
odds, they agree to go forth with the wedding and continue to

set the table and dress for the occasion. Nelly dresses for what she expects will be the biggest day of her life, convinced that her fiancé will appear.

Summary (extract)

From her bedroom, narcoleptic **Nelly** (thirty years old) can overhear the conversations about her from underneath the floorboards. Isolated from her family and the world around her, she begins to question her sanity and existence. This is the first time in the play that we hear **Nelly**'s desperation for a world outside the prison that is her bedroom. The expected arrival of her soon-to-be-husband is her ticket away from the confines of this lonely world.

Nelly   Next Friday? … Next Friday in Berdawnay … to eat
kneffay … There's no one left! There's only me! I'm always
sleepy! Naked in the middle of the war! What do they all have to
shout about? They must think my fiancé isn't going to come, so
they've left. (*Shouting.*) Hey, my fiancé is going to come! They
don't hear me, they think I'm still asleep. Maybe I actually am
asleep this very moment. 'But you're here, Nelly! With your eyes
open.' I don't know anymore. 'You don't know anymore if you're
dreaming or not?' No, Nelly, I don't know anymore. Before, in
my dreams, I'd sometimes turn into a big tree; I'd catch fire in the
middle of a wood, I'd run with all my roots and throw myself over
a cliff. Then I would wake up. 'You would wake up?' Yes, I would
wake up and I would know what the words 'waking up' meant:
finding a peaceful blue sky, a world very different from the one in
my dreams, and then yes, I would know that I'd been dreaming
and that I had just woken up. 'And now?' Now? 'No, no, don't
cry, Nelly.' I can't! Now all I dream about is the toilet, the door
and the concrete wall. And when I wake up, I see the same door,
Nelly, the same concrete wall, that's it. Now I no longer know
where I am Nelly. Can you help me? 'I can't do anything. Nelly.
Nothing.'

Forties +

From

CATEGORY B

by Roy Williams

Category B was first performed as part of the 'Not Black and White' season at the Tricycle Theatre, London on 8 October 2009, directed by Paulette Randall with the following cast: Sharon Duncan-Brewster (Angela), Kobna Holdbrook-Smith (David), Aml Ameen (Rio), Robert Whitelock (Andy), Jimmy Akingbola (Saul), Abhin Galeya (Riz), Karl Collins (Errol), Jaye Griffiths (Chandra) and John Boyega (Reece).

British playwright Roy Williams focuses his attention on Category B prison to create a chilling drama which exposes the hypocrisies, corruption and criminal activities carried out by the inmates and the prison officers. Set in the present day at the fictional Thames Gate Prison in London, the play responds to the overcrowding in UK prisons, which has almost doubled over the last twenty years. The increase of prisoners has had a significant impact on Category B prisons, the first place prisoners are sent after they have been convicted, resulting in a melting pot of extremely dangerous criminals in the same place as first-time petty offenders, who are both unable to be placed in the correct facility due to a shortage of cells. Throughout Williams's play we experience the prison system through the eyes of the senior prison officers as they struggle to maintain some authority and control in an almost impossible environment. Needless to say, Category B prison remains a place that is despised by both convicts and prison officers alike.

Senior prison officer, Angela, has no tolerance for 'bent' screws (prison officers) who break the prison rules by meddling in dodgy dealings with inmates. So when she's informed by the prison snitch Errol, a repeat offender, about a screw allowing mobile phones into the prison in exchange for money, she makes it her mission to find the culprit.

But that's not the only thing on Angela's mind. The new prison officer, David Saunders, has just arrived from Category D at Rainesworth Prison (referred to by Angela as the Hilton in comparison to Category B) hungry for the challenge of working in Category B. New inmates are coming in thick and fast and as her failing loveless marriage plummets further into dissolution, Angela struggles to maintain her undercover love affair with fellow officer Andy.

The only thing that has remained constant is the trusted and, arguably, the most dangerous inmate on the wing, Saul, who has succeeded in keeping the prisoners in the C wing in line, to the benefit of Angela and the understaffed prison guards, who reward his efforts by turning a blind eye to the drug trafficking and drug use within the prison walls. But as Errol counts down the days to his release, Saul is looking for a number two and has his eyes on Errol, to Angela's disapproval.

At the centre of the story is the relationship between new inmate and first-time offender Rio, convicted for gang rape, and repeat offender Errol. When Rio's mum unexpectedly pays a visit to Errol asking him to protect her child, the plot thickens as Rio discovers that Errol is his father. Despite Rio's mother's efforts, her action to call on his father to protect him proves to be the wrong decision. A death in the prison cell leaves Rio in hot water, Andy revealed as the bent screw and Errol a free man.

Summary (extract)

Angela (black, early forties) talks directly to the audience to deliver this speech. Drug dealer **Riz**, who **Saul** suspects has been stealing from him, has been found dead in his prison cell. **Angela** takes this moment to share her greatest fears about her job.

Angela My husband Joel asked me once, what is it that I fear most about my job. My answer, opening the doors. Cell doors to be precise. In the mornings, when they are let out. You see, during the night, when they are all tucked up, it is the only time when we cannot keep an eye on them. They have eight or nine hours alone to do God knows what to each other and to themselves. And believe me they do. We had this one crazy, he strips himself naked, rubs his own faeces and his cellmate's faeces all over his body, before slashing his own wrists with a razor blade. See, his thinking is we would be less likely to try and save him. And he was right, in another life was I going anywhere near him. One of our lot tried, played the hero, he managed to stop the bleeding, that is when he wasn't throwing up every five seconds. In case you are wondering, that prisoner died. And all the Governor cares about is protecting his own arse. Did we do everything we could to save him, did we follow procedure by the book? Never mind that young screw who might have caught God know what off that man. Now normally when something like that goes down, at the end of the shift we all take each other down the nearest boozer, knock them back until there's no tomorrow. We keep knocking them back until today's events seem like a vague distant memory in our minds. That's how it go. Screws United! We are there for each other, ca no one is there for us. I shoulda bin larging it with those lot, going blind on double vodkas, but my man Joel has been bitchin it 24/7 lately about how I'm hardly ever home these days. I come home that night to find Joel, sitting on his fat arse again, watching TV with the kids, without it once entering his head to have dinner ready for me. After all this chat. I blow my mates out, for this! That is how much I am valued in my own home. He has the front to ask me how my day was. And he wonders why he hasn't been getting *any* lately. So, I cooked dinner, and waited, until everyone around the table had their mouths full of spaghetti bolognese, when I told them about me seeing a six-foot man killing himself while covered in his own shit that is dripping off him from head to toe. Now who would feel like eating their spaghetti bolognese after hearing a story like that? So, you will understand when I say, me walking into the shower room, seeing a man strangled, all dead up, is no big thing. In fact, it is a luxury.

From

THE USUAL AUNTIJIES

by Paven Virk

The *Usual Auntijies* was first performed at the Belgrade Theatre,
Coventry, UK on 5 March 2011, directed by Barry Kyle with the
following cast: Shelley King (Aunty 5), Shalini Peiris (Gurpreet),
Jamila Massey (Aunty 4), Mamta Kaash (Aunty 2) and Pushpinder
Chani (Raj).

British playwright Paven Virk's comic drama pulls at the
heartstrings. Written in Punjabi and English, *The Usual
Auntijies* comprises a collection of love stories based on real-life
experiences from the unheard and often disregarded female voices
of the South Asian elderly community. *The Usual Auntijies* deals
with themes such as forced marriages, vulnerable adults (in
particular, autism), loss and domestic violence. The glue which
holds all these stories together comes in the form of a poem by the
celebrated Punjabi poet Jasvir Kang, whose poem 'Dolli (Wedding
Carriage)' forces the women to re-evaluate their situation, giving
them the strength and impetus to move forward.

The play takes place in a home for abused women: three retired
elders reveal the dark and painful stories behind their physical
scars, loneliness and heartbreak. Meanwhile, just down the street,
a young newly-wed Indian bride has taken residence in her
husband's family home, opening her world to relentless abuse. By
the course of the play we are taken on a journey of enlightenment
as the women overcome their demons and learn to embrace love,
empowerment and a new lease of freedom.

The Usual Auntijies is set somewhere in the city, shining a light
on two very different households. Aunty 5, a dominant and
mischievous South Asian elderly woman who resides at number
23, a refuge for abused women, spends her days pottering around
the home speaking with her beloved green dove (a rare breed of
bird found in India), correcting Aunty 2 on her poor articulation of
the English language and fantasizing about becoming Joan Collins
from her favourite prime-time television soap opera, *Dynasty*.

Aunty 2, simply dressed in a traditional salwar kameez, is the designated cook in the house, cooking traditional Indian recipes to bring comfort and reignite memories of home. But her dreams transport her far away from India and Britain as she imagines a new life in Greece, away from her husband whose domestic abuse has left an inerasable severe burn mark on her face and overwhelming feelings of guilt.

Despite Aunty 2's best efforts, Aunty 5 struggles to bond and open up to her, blaming the reason on the language barrier. But we soon discover that her best friend, Aunty 4, has left the home. Aunty 5 is convinced that she has nothing to learn from Aunty 2, but when Aunty 2 recites Jasvir's poem 'Dolli' in Punjabi and then in English, Aunty 5 starts to realize that they may have more things in common than she initially thought.

The poem travels via radio into the house at number 31. Gurpreet, a newly-wed in her late teens, listens intently to the words, which are silenced by her autistic husband Raj, who turns the radio off. Gurpreet's life reflects the words in the poem, she suffers in silence while dealing with Raj's emotionally charged outbursts, as well as being subjected to physical abuse from his immediate family. The worlds between the two generations of South Asian women collide when Aunty 5 spots Gurpreet on the park bench holding her belongings in a plastic carrier bag and immediately recognizes another victim of abuse. After sharing a few words of wisdom and advice, Gurpreet calls Aunty 5 'Auntijie'. (The 'ji' in the term is traditionally used after someone's name as a sign of respect; it is also sometimes used to address women older than oneself.) Aunty 5 is touched and offers Gurpreet a place at the home. Gurpreet returns back home to her husband with a gift from Aunty 5: her beloved bird.

Back at number 23, the strained relationship between Aunty 5 and Aunty 2 is interrupted by Aunty 4, who arrives at the home bloodied, bruised and calling out for husband Baldev. The women assume that Aunty 4 is a victim of domestic violence, but instead she discloses how a spontaneous family road trip with her husband and son (as a reward for being such a good wife) ended in tragedy, leaving Aunty 4 returning to the refuge, the only survivor of a car accident.

As the play develops, Aunty 5 appears more like Joan Collins, trading in her Indian suit for a bright jacket with huge shoulder pads, a pencil skirt, frilly silk blouse and killer black heels. Disguising her Scottish-Indian accent for an imitation of Alexis's accent, she goes so far as to call herself Joan. Only when she is fully transformed can she find the strength to reveal her story to Aunty 2.

By the end of the play, each character is forced to acknowledge and begin to deal with the trauma in their life. Raj gives Gurpreet a suitcase to pack her belongings and leave the house. But when Gurpreet arrives at number 23 with a suitcase and the caged bird, all is not what it seems. This is a play about love, friendship and letting go.

Summary (extract)

Time has passed since **Aunty 5** transformed into Joan Collins; she still wears her new outfit, but her hair is now short and dyed black and her accent has probably returned to its normal Scottish-Indian. She sits on a park bench with the bird cage on her lap, preparing to release the bird forever. **Gurpreet** enters holding a carrier bag and looking lost. She sits next to Aunty 5, feeding the pigeons with chapattis. **Aunty 5** recognizes an abused woman when she sees one, and reveals the reason why she left her husband to encourage **Gurpreet** to do the same.

Aunty 5   Dear, I wouldn't encourage them. Here I am trying to release one and there you are trying to gather them around.

[…]

You can't understand a word I'm saying can you? Pity. I have so many thoughts and no one to share them with. There was one but she left me. Chose the company of a beast over me. We just don't leave our husbands, no matter how badly they treat you. But I would never return.

Beat.

The day I left I saw a young English couple holding hands. They were going up the escalator and I was going down. As soon as I got to the bottom I felt a short of breath, like my journey was coming to an end and before I knew it I was on their escalator. I followed them shop after shop. Is this what two people in love look like? Two birds flying around each other? Two mountains overlooking each other? I couldn't keep up, but I couldn't lose them. I needed to get close to this word *love*, so I looked it up in the dictionary but it only told me the meaning.

[…]

Then I caught my reflection in the mirror. I saw a plain salwar kameez, long straight black hair and creamy skin. I looked closer, my kameez loose and baggy, so not to show off my body. My hair unkempt with even more grey hairs than my own mother. My skin heavy with dark circles and my eyes sore from crying myself to sleep. But the truly sad thing was, when I walked down the street, to me I looked no different from all the other women. Our women. The only difference was, I had set myself free and not realised. You silly woman, you are free. Like Joan Collins. Free to rule your dynasty. Free to conquer your demons.

Aunty 5 *looks at* **Gurpreet**.

You look like all the others. May I give you some words of wisdom? You see to be a strong independent woman, you must know the secret …

[…]

Give me your hand.

Aunty 5 *gestures hand.*

Hand.

[…]

The secret is …

Aunty 5 *places* **Gurpreet**'s *hand on her shoulder.*

… shoulder pads.

Beat.

Please, give them a good squeeze.

From

THE HOUR OF FEELING

by Mona Mansour

The Hour of Feeling received its first UK staged reading at the
HighTide Festival, Halesworth, Suffolk, on 6 May 2012, directed
by Richard Fitch with the following cast: Ishia Bennison (Beder),
Robert Gilbert (Adham), Sofia Stuart (Abir), Geoffrey Breton
(George), Jack Cosgrove (Theo) and Olivia Vinall (Diana).

Mona Mansour's play tackles the subject of identity and
displacement to question if a person can ever fully renounce their
identity, in the same way that one can renounce their faith. The
play is set in the summer of 1967 moments before the historic
Six-Day War between Israel and the nearby states: Jordan,
Syria and Egypt. Its lead character Adham, a young Palestinian
academic from the university in Cairo, wants nothing more than to
completely immerse himself in white English society. With a love
of English Romantic poetry, he quickly falls for a French-Arabic-
speaking liberal young woman named Abir, who shares the same
passion for the Western world. Despite his mother's reservations,
Adham marries Abir. When Adham receives an invitation to speak
at University College London, the newly-weds readily seize the
opportunity to leave Beit Hanina – a village considered a 'suburb'
of East Jerusalem, captured by Jordanian forces – and Adham's
mother and head to London.

In London the newly-weds' relationship is put to the ultimate
test. Before Adham can deliver his career-defining lecture on
Romantic literature, he is expected at the delegates' lunch for
an informal introduction. Keen to impress his fellow British
professors, he spends the entire lunch dismissing his wife, whose
lack of the English language and determination to speak in Arabic
becomes an irksome embarrassment. But his young, strong-willed,
opinionated wife refuses to be silenced, gaining support from
English scholar Theo, a non-fluent Arabic speaker. To make things
worse, one of the academics asks Adham a question to which he
struggles to find an intellectual response. The lunch culminates

with an imagined appearance from Adham's mother, a strong, intense woman who berates her son for his poor choice of wife and for falling short in the conversation with the academics, considering her efforts to give him the best education.

Adham pulls it all together in time to deliver the best lecture of his life. A conversation with scholars at the after-party reveals the recent news coverage on the start of the Six-Day War. Abir regrets leaving the family with the war approaching and is adamant to return home. But Adham has his sights on a possible fellowship in London – his ticket to a life away from the borders of Israel and war. The only question remains: is he prepared to abandon his mother as well as his wife for freedom?

Summary (extract)

Beder (Palestinian, **Adham**'s mother, fifty years old) is described by the author as world-weary but fierce and funny too. **Beder** is meeting her son's girlfriend for the first time. She is unimpressed with his choice, considering **Abir** a peasant girl, unfit for the apple of her eye. Talk turns to **Adham**'s success and the sacrifices she made along the way.

Beder   When the Quakers opened the new school, I begged
them to let him in. We couldn't afford more than him being a day
student. He was so frightened the first time I took him there.

[...]

You remember?

[...]

Who knows [why he was afraid]. He'd been at the little village
school before that. This one was farther away, toward Ramallah.
We had to take a bus every day. There's the entrance, where the
gate is. Then you have to go down these stone steps, and you're
on a path between a grove of fig trees, the school building in the
distance. Well. I get him there and he starts crying. And I am
thinking, who is this child? What is wrong with him? So fearful!
Did I make him this way?

[...]

Then he tells me: he thinks bandits are going to come from behind
the trees and slit his throat. You remember?

[...]

And I'm thinking, what to do? I can't send him away like this, his
face covered in tears. So I make it a game. This wasn't my nature,
this kind of whimsical approach.

[...]

I say, Do you see this sign, my son? This entrance to the school?
This is a magical entrance. Once you go through these gates, you
are safe. Just be careful as you walk these first few steps. He was
always running, everywhere. They used very old stones when they
built the school. They say these were from the front steps of the
great hall that housed Alexander the Great.

[...]

We walked through the gate, and I take your hand, and the wind
came up. I say, 'Do you feel yourself drifting, as you take this
walk?' Because none of us was ever allowed to drift, really. 'Let

yourself drift, my son, as the ancient grove makes way for you. The trees will blow to you. See? Each one nods! Each one says, this is a scholar!' Each tree had a name, do you remember this?

[…]

And you look at me, and you look at the trees, and you say: 'Tell me then. Tell me each tree's name.' This is when I realize, this boy has exceptional intelligence. Such imagination.

[…]

And I think, quickly: what is the name of each tree? And I say: 'Al-Mutanabbi, the great poet. Al-Yajizi. Al-Barudi. Aristotle. Shakespeare.' You see? And then you took a breath, and you walked, and you let go of my hand, and it was like I was barely there.

[…]

There's one thing I never told you, part of this story. I wanted to walk you all the way down the steps, through the trees. I wanted to take you inside the building, and sit next to you, and sit there all day to make sure we were getting our money's worth! I wanted nothing more than to take you all the way in. It was the last thing in the world I wanted, to leave you to go down those steps alone. But I had to. I stood there and watched you go.

[…]

You know what I did after I left you? I came home and I threw away every picture I had of your brother. […] I had very few to begin with. Baby pictures. […] Tore them to bits, each, and then, yes.

[…]

The way I felt with you on the steps. This – feeling this –

She puts her hand on her chest: a pang she doesn't have words for.

This was – this was the same way I felt every time I looked at those pictures. Anyway, I couldn't stand to look at them anymore. What does that emotion serve? It's going to help me get your brother out of Lebanon, rescue him? I knew that if I got rid of him, his pictures, I could do anything. I knew that to get you where you needed to go, all such feelings would have to be gotten rid of.

From

ARCHIPELAGO

by Caridad Svich

Archipelago received its world premiere at the Ilkhom Theater of Mark Weil in Tashkent, Uzbekistan, produced by Irina Bharat and Tyler Polomsky for the spring 2014 Festival of American Work. The play was translated into Russian for this production by Oksana Aleshina and directed by the artistic director of the theatre Boris Gafurov, with the following cast: Olga Volodina (H) and Maxim Fadeev (B). *Archipelago* was a nominee for the Kilroys' 2014 THE LIST for Best New Plays.

Svich's writing style could be likened to the work of Debbie Tucker Green, Sarah Kane, Samuel Beckett, a master of language and thus a genius in engaging the audience with the nothing more than a vague setting, choppy sentences and powerful monologues.

Archipelago is greater than a play with themes, as it is more preoccupied with understanding humanity through an exploration of the strength and fragility of the human mind. Rightfully referred to as a memory play, Svich playfully focuses her play on the act of memory, the obsession to create and revisit fond memories, as well as the inability to control our memories as a result of aging, trauma or dementia; a complete wipe out of an entire lifetime of memories.

The relationship between the two characters in the play is anchored by their shared memories, which over the course of the play acts as both a comfort and irritation. From being lovers on a bridge, to days of slumming through the city, squatting and living off a diet of gummy critters and chips out of machines the couple continue to navigate their relationship through times of austerity and war avoiding bombs and bullets along the way.

Against these bleak times, their differences become apparent which results in them losing each other for the first time. But as faith would have it, years later, they are reunited.

But just as things begin to look brighter, a tragedy occurs, resulting in a coma which threatens to separate the couple for good.

Summary

After losing each other for the first time, the couple have found each other several years later. But as they slip into a place of familiarity and happiness, a gunshot leaves B falling to the ground and H left in darkness.

This monologue by H has been extracted from the beginning of the next scene entitled Forgetting (2nd Leaving).

H   You think you know how you're going to react when
A gun pierces through the skin and bone of someone you care for,
But the fact is, you don't know at all.

What you want to do is scream at someone,
Be inappropriate,
Say all the wrong things.
But what you do
Is cry and stare
And forget all the right words.

Blank. You become a blank.
The world turns grey,
And hatred fills every pore of your body,
Because it should've been me.
It should be me there in the hospital
Not him. Not like this.

Where's prayer now?

He was in a coma.
Would be for some time, they said,
While the guns raged outside.
Thought: what happened to the fucking ceasefire?

I wanted to use his words. I wanted to curse just like him.
Fucking, fucking …

But I didn't say anything.
I was useless.
And it fucking hurt.

A moment.

They said I was there for days and days and days.
Waiting, drinking weak tea,
Filling my stomach with acidity.
They said I was fine,
And that there was nothing more they could tell me about him
And his situation anymore.
They used that word: 'situation'
As if they were talking about an episode on TV.

I shouted.
Fucking, fucking …

A nurse handed me some pills.
'It will help you with the shock. Take two of these with water, and everything will pass.'

Imagine the power of these pills, I thought, that with only a glass of water,
I will stop feeling everything.

I tossed the pills into the trash
And went out the hospital
Past all the staff and screaming babies
And women and children with broken limbs
And hard-working people doing their job of maintaining life.

Breath.

For a moment, I tried to remember what he had said to me
Before he ran out of the cave.
Before we thought the world was a little bit safer again.
But the fact was, I couldn't remember.

I couldn't remember

All I could see was his back
Blood gushing …
And the horrible, whimpering sound his body made
As he …

Thought: where did it come from?
Who in fucking hell fired that gun?

No one knew
The phrase was: Nobody was seen.

It was a magic bullet, then,
That somehow found its way into his …

I wanted to scream. Like the good lapsed Christian soul that I was.
But I just looked up
Into the sky

And dreamt of leaving.

Today. Right now. First plane you can find.

I am no good at this.
Sorry.
I am shit at hospitals.
Sorry.
I can't be here anymore.
Sorry.
Sorry.
Sorry.

(and I know I'll be saying Sorry for the rest of my life)

As I touched his palm
And he, barely a pulse,
Barely
576 hours since …

A moment.
The airport was a zoo. Security was fucking hell.
I waited in the queue until finally
The boarding gate was opened.
A man in a linen jacket said.
'You look like you're sleepwalking.'
I didn't answer.
Couldn't think of anything.

Thirty thousand feet up in the air
I dreamt of his face:
The curve of his lips,
The tender slope of his nose,
The crinkly little lines that had set in near his eyes.
Lines of worry, I thought, or fatigue.
We all get them sooner or later.
Thought: how he seemed in some ways just the same
Exactly
As when we used to drift through stations and bars and beautiful
young things.
But really, really he wasn't at all …

When I went to the desert, I was seeking escape I think,
Or a sense of peace?
Not holiness. Not ceremony. None of the usual things.
My life was discordant, adrift, unsettled.
Still is, actually.
But at that time I thought a trip might just, just change things.

When I saw him again
Everything rushed back into my brain:
Moments we'd spent,
How he would hold me,
The stupid silly things we'd say to each other,
Weird cravings – chips and gummy critters and lemon fizzies …

How could I have walked away all those years ago?
What had made me so damned angry?

And then, up in the air,
His face came to me again.

What the fuck am I doing?
I should go back.
But we were already at the thirty-six-thousand mark,
And the seat belt sign was off.

Publications

The House That Will Not Stand by Marcus Gardley. Methuen Drama. ISBN 978-1-4742-2884-8

Melody Loses Her Mojo by Keith Saha. Methuen Drama. ISBN: 978-1-4725-2442-3

The Methuen Drama Book of Post-Black Plays edited by Harry J. Elam Jr and Douglas A. Jones Jr: *Bulrusher* by Eisa Davis, *Good Goods* by Christina Anderson, *The Shipment* by Young Jean Lee, *Satellites* by Diana Son, *... And Jesus Moonwalks the Mississippi* by Marcus Gardley, *Antebellum* by Robert O'Hara, *In the Continuum* by Danai Gurira and Nikkole Salter and *Black Diamond* by J. Nicole Brooks. Methuen Drama. ISBN: 978-1-4081-7382-4

Ruined by Lynn Nottage. Nick Hern Books. ISBN: 978-1-84842-088-5

My Name is ... by Sudha Bhuchar. Methuen Drama. ISBN: 978-1-4725-8833-3

Child of the Divide by Sudha Bhuchar. Methuen Drama: ISBN: 978-0-4137-7613-6

Alaska by DC Moore. Methuen Drama. ISBN: 978-0-7136-8822-1

The Fish Eyes Trilogy by Anita Majumdar. *Fish Eyes*, *Boys With Cars* and *Let Me Borrow That Top*. Playwrights Canada Press. ISBN: 978-1-7709-1327-1

Blood by Emteaz Hussain. Methuen Drama. ISBN: 978-1-4742-5079-5

Shades by Alia Bano. Methuen Drama. ISBN: 978-1-4081-1523-7

At Her Feet by Nadia Davids. Oshun Books. ISBN: 978-1-7700-7055-4

Josephine and I by Cush Jumbo. Methuen Drama. ISBN: 978-1-4725-3453-8

Katori Hall Plays 1: Hoodoo Love, Saturday Night/Sunday Morning, The Mountaintop, Hurt Village. Methuen Drama. ISBN: 978-1-4081-4702-3

We Are Proud to Present ... by Jackie Sibblies Drury. Methuen Drama. ISBN: 978-1-4725-8509-7

Black Jesus by Anders Lustgarten. Methuen Drama. ISBN: 978-1-4725-2747-9

The Westbridge by Rachel De-lahay. Methuen Drama. ISBN: 978-1-4081-7201-8

Gurpreet Kaur Bhatti Plays 1: Behsharam (Shameless), Behzti, Behud, Fourteen, Khandan. Oberon Books. ISBN: 978-1-7831-9130-7

The Fever Chart: Three Visions of the Middle East by Naomi Wallace. Theatre Communications Group. ISBN: 978-1-5593-6337-2

Crash by Pamela Mala Sinha. Scirocco Drama. ISBN: 978-1-8972-8999-0

American Next Wave: Four Contemporary Plays from the HighTide Festival: *Perish* by Stella Fawn Ragsdale, *The Hour of Feeling* by Mona Mansour, *Bethany* by Laura Marks, *Neighbors* by Branden Jacobs-Jenkins. Methuen Drama. ISBN: 978-1-4081-7309-1

Fireworks: Al' Ab Nariya by Dalia Taha. Methuen Drama. ISBN: 978-1-4742-4450-3

Talk To Me: Monologue Plays edited by Eric Lane and Nina Shengold. Includes *Tamam* by Betty Shamieh. Vintage. ISBN: 978-1-4000-7615-4

Salaam. Peace: An Anthology of Middle Eastern-American Drama edited by Holly Hill and Dina Amin: *Ten Acrobats in an Amazing Leap of Faith* by Yussef El Guindi, *9 Parts of Desire* by Heather Raffo, *Desert Sunrise* by Misha Shulman, *Browntown* by Sam Younis, *The Black Eyed* by Betty Shamieh. Theatre Communications Group. ISBN: 978-1-5593-6332-7

I Just Stopped By To See The Man by Stephen Jeffreys. Nick Hern Books. ISBN: 978-1-8545-9482-2

Chef by Sabrina Mahfouz. Methuen Drama. ISBN: 978-1-4742-6539-3

Harlem Duet by Djanet Sears. Scirocco Drama. ISBN: 978-1-8962-3927-9

A Day at the Racists by Anders Lustgarten. Methuen Drama. ISBN: 978-1-4081-3058-2

The Husbands by Sharmila Chauhan. Oberon Books. ISBN: 978-1-7831-9113-0

A Canadian Monsoon by Sheila James. Playwrights Union of Canada. ISBN: 978-1-5529-0037-6

Rice Boy by Sunil Kuruvilla. 2nd edition. Playwrights Canada Press. ISBN: 978-0-8875-4672-3

The Beloved by Amir Nizar Zuabi. Methuen Drama. ISBN: 978-1-4081-7315-2

Oh My Sweet Land by Amir Nizar Zuabi. Methuen Drama. ISBN: 978-1-4725-8939-2

Wedding Day at the Cro-Magnons by Wajdi Mouawad. Oberon Books. ISBN: 978-1-8400-2848-5

Roy Williams Plays: 4: Sucker Punch; Category B; Joe Guy; Baby Girl; There's Only One Wayne Matthews. Methuen Drama. ISBN: 978-1-4725-2069-2

The Usual Auntijies by Paven Virk. Methuen Drama. ISBN: 978-1-4081-5217-1